PAINTING

made easy

PAINTING

made easy

By JOHN MILLS

GRAMERCY PUBLISHING COMPANY : NEW YORK

CONTENTS

The publishers wish to thank the Trustees, the National Gallery, London, for permission to reproduce the paintings on pages 32, 49, 97, 114 and 116, and the Trustees, The Tate Gallery, London, for permission to reproduce the paintings on pages 98, 99 and 120.

I

SEEING A PICTURE

Before you start to paint, you will find it both rewarding and helpful to study the work of the great artists of the present and the past. On the shelves of your home may be some of the wonderful art reproduction books that are being published today, and from the beautiful colored plates you can glean a great deal of valuable information. Better still, if you live in or near a town that has an art gallery, spend an afternoon or two going through it. The first time, make a mental or an actual note of the picture or pictures which strike you most forcibly, and then later take time to study them. If possible, sit down opposite them and absorb what the artist has said.

The professional painter has given years of his life to studying and perfecting his craft. Not only does he become technically a master of his brushes and colors but also, parallel with this achievement, his mind becomes more alert and he sees much that the average person misses. It is this seeing *more* that is really the keynote of his genius. By constantly studying and working, the artist, whether he is a writer, a musician or a painter, climbs a mountain which gives him a greater view than that of others. By his works he passes on to others what he has seen. His talent enables him to draw from an often complicated scene the elements of a great composition. His sensitivity will enable him to build these into a fine picture, balanced in color and shape.

The keen perception of the artist is a talent, but it is one which you, too, can cultivate. As a beginning student, you need to be constantly aware of all that is around you. Not only should you make practical notes in a sketch book, but also your eye must always be ready to take in subtleties that are often half-hidden: reflections in water, their tone and color values; the pure, strong colors of a sunset or the deep tones of the troughs in a stormy sea. You will not understand or learn these things in a day. Rather, you will begin to perceive thoroughly the objects around you only after years of practice. Do not be discouraged, however, by these warning sentences—their intent is to encourage you, to ask you to look as deeply and patiently as time will allow. Even a simple scene from nature, when seen and placed in its correct arrangement on the canvas, will bring you intense satisfaction.

Try to study some of the wonderful little pictures produced by the Dutch School of the sixteenth and seventeenth centuries to gain an insight into the artistic use of light, reflection and reflected colors. These small delicate paintings are masterpieces of humble and sincere application of skill. The handling of the light source and of shadow and figure arrangement classes many of them with the greatest paintings in the world.

The French Impressionists, working in the last century, used entirely new and revolutionary techniques of color, composition and light. Such men as Claude Monet first pointed to the beauties of shadow in snow or the low-tone harmonies of such humdrum places as railway stations and muddy country lanes.

When looking at a picture try to visualize the actual scene from which the painter must have worked. Whether it was the wide-open French countryside or a small-roomed interior of Holland, or a dramatic allegorical composition of one of the great Italian masters, such as Titian, Tintoretto and Botticelli, try to imagine how *you* might have dealt with such a subject. Simplify these scenes. Perhaps even make small sketches embodying the principal components of some of them. Give some time to such exercises. This will teach you much about composition—that is, how to fit the principal objects into a picture area—and how the masters built up their paintings, not from minute details but from strong basic shapes underlying the whole.

If possible, compare the treatment of the same type of scene by different artists: a snow scene by Peter Breughel the Elder and one by Gustave Courbet; a seascape by one of the Van der Veldes and one by Boudin; a portrait by Holbein and one by Renoir. In all cases the artist will be seeking to express his thought and his particular approach. Sometimes the result may be tempered to the fashion of the day or to the order of a patron, but largely each picture is an individual accomplishment. It is up to you to decide what you feel about each artist's work. Personal taste can be cultivated, but it should never be dictated.

As important as the study of actual paintings is the possession of a small pocket sketch book. This need not be very big; there is one on the market about 5 inches high by 7 inches long, which you can carry in your pocket or handbag. Also, try always to carry two or three pencils and, if possible, a penknife. The habit of using a sketch book cannot be started too soon. Be it ever so tiny or fragmentary, the sketch is very important to a painter. It can provide ideas which at a later date you may want to incorporate in pictures, or to enlarge into full-sized compositions. The thumbnail sketch, so named apparently by William Hogarth, who is supposed at one time in his career to have actually sketched two figures fighting on his thumbnail, need not be very detailed. It can be as rough as you like as long as it captures the essentials of the scene before you.

The sketch in Fig. 1 (page 14) shows a brief outline of a scene that might have been glimpsed from a hotel window in a small port. Looking down across the dock, there is a medium-sized cargo ship unloading, while across the river is an outline of an industrial district. Those few simple lines give the skeleton for an interesting composition. Quite obviously, the foreground could be enlivened further, by adding a truck or, if you wanted to be more elaborate, a railway siding with trucks ready to receive the crates being un-

Fig. 1

loaded from the hold of the ship. Downriver, behind the vessel, you could place a busy little tug pulling a string of barges, a small sailboat or another steamer going up to her berth. The distant range of buildings and chimneys need not have any further elaboration. If you leave them as a single-tone backdrop, they will serve to give distance, and will also add character to the general scene.

In contrast, the second sketch (Fig. 2) could represent almost any country scene. A narrow country road winds off into the

Fig. 2

distance, in all probability leading to the small village. Do not overdo this kind of subject, for if you should be tempted to add more buildings in the foreground or perhaps vehicles on the road, or to work out the fence too minutely, you would lose the feeling of spaciousness, of being out in the open air. Your effect can be attained very simply with as few lines as possible. Rely largely on the greens which you will use on the fields; the nearer they come, the brighter they will be; the farther they recede, the bluer and paler they will become. The little buildings do not need great detail. Carefully drawn windows, slates, tiles and blocks of stone will only make the picture fussy and constricted. Keep everything as simple as possible. You have only to look at a distant village to see how little the eye can actually pick out a quarter or half a mile away.

The third example (Fig. 3), lends itself to extremely imaginative treatment. You can have a great deal of fun with a fairground,

Fig. 3

possibly showing it at night. The shapes are wonderful—the whirling carousel in the foreground, with its waistlike tower; the big Ferris wheel, tents, flags, balloons. All kinds of strange, out-of-the-way objects and vivid colors can come into a picture based on a few little scribbled notes taken at a fair.

When undertaking a nighttime scene, it is wise to take careful mental notes of the colors. Then write down as accurately as possible the colors in your paintbox which you think you would use to mix those needed for the picture. For example, the sky would not be just dark blue. Don't forget, at a fair everything is lighted with a tremendous variety of blue, red and green lights, and all these combined throw a lurid glare into the sky which

15

produces a rather crimson, purplish effect at the top of the picture and, lower down, becomes a form of ruddy glow. Don't worry if at first you can't catch movement. If you are too exact in your drawing, for example, trying to depict every link of the chains swinging the chairs around, you will miss the over-all action. Your eye sees the flying chain only as a blur. So, broadly and boldly draw in your principal lines and your basic shapes. Don't spoil the freshness by trying too hard to put in every last detail.

Often, quite unexpectedly, you will come up against an arrangement of shapes, a lighting effect, or some strange conglomeration of objects that suggests a picture to you. So, whip out your sketch book; get down those details. Otherwise, "out of sight, out of mind." Your own breakfast table, for example, may inspire you. Perhaps one morning a vase of flowers, a teapot, your egg and bacon are in an especially attractive position, and you suddenly feel that the pieces fall into place as a composition which interests you. The milk bottle and the bowl of flowers balance each other, and give a feeling of stability to the teapot in the middle. See Fig. 4.

Fig. 4

In a picture like this, lighting is important. In fact, lighting is important in any painting. But in an arrangement of a group of objects, termed a "still life," the direction of the light is a first consideration. Here, it was probably coming from about 45 degrees away on the right, lighting up first the milk bottle, then the right-hand side of the teapot, and throwing a deep shadow across the cloth. In drawing the bowl of flowers delineate light and shade carefully to give it a feeling of body and depth.

Working in still life may appear a rather dull and uninteresting business, but actually you will find that it is one of the finest ways of learning to paint and draw. For one thing, your model is static. The light won't change, the colors remain the same, and there are no fleeting clouds to obscure, darken or lighten the whole scene. Also, as you proceed with your work, you will be amazed at the hidden subtleties of reflected light, of reflected color and of shape. You will develop a sense of proportion, learn how to obtain symmetry (by drawing both sides of a pot, for example), and how to represent different textures (the shiny glaze of the teapot, the smooth glass of the milk bottle and the rough weave of the tablecloth).

It might also be fun to paint a scene similar to that shown in Fig. 5. It may be a night or evening experience, as was the fair. Perhaps, walking along the street, you suddenly come upon lines of people waiting to get into a theatre. This would make an

Fig. 5

interesting painting; you have the brilliant rectangle of the opening of the theatre itself contrasted with the dark walls around it and the crowds of people waiting to go in. It is surprising how people's faces seem to shine at night. Their clothes, their bodies become almost indistinguishable, and often your effect can be achieved quite simply by concentrating on the little ovals of brightness in various shades of flesh color. The theatre front itself cannot be too bright. Keep your colors as light in tone as you possibly can, to get the maximum contrast between this brightly lighted part and the cool, dark tones of the surrounding buildings.

These examples are intended only as suggestions for your sketch book. Learn to use it regularly to stimulate your memory. No matter how rough the drawings, you will find, even a year or two afterward, that you can not only see the whole scene again, but you can also hear it. If you don't have a chance to use your sketches soon after you made them, don't worry. Like good wine, sketches mature with the passing months and even years. Sometimes you will be able to use your rough drawings as the basis of a better picture than you could have done with the scene before your eyes. The unimportant details will have receded from memory, but your sketch will provide you with the essential materials for your picture.

In adapting a sketch to a painting you need not use, for example, exactly the sky which you saw at the time of making the sketch. That is the beauty of painting and drawing; you are not a camera; you are not trying to take a photograph. A painter can select, can borrow. He can put two or three sketches together and make a picture. The only thing he is going to be judged by is his final result.

II

IMAGINATION AND COMPOSITION

As a painter faced with a model—whether it is a bowl of flowers, a landscape or seascape—you must first of all solve the problem of what you want to say about it. The final picture is what counts; how you obtain it is your personal problem. As we pointed out in the preceding chapter, an artist is not a camera, and in many ways he will fail if he attempts to emulate the camera. Overconcern with minute details and overworking of the picture will very often make the finished result a lifeless, dull product.

When you set out, whether it is for your first attempt or for any picture, try automatically to see your painting as a whole, apart from its present surroundings, framed and on the wall. The successful composition is one that will sit quite happily in the frame; and, when it is looked at, will not give the appearance of smallness or meanness, of seeming to fall downward, or of having slipped to one side.

Composition is one of the principal problems for the painter: how to transpose successfully from nature into the constricting shape of the frame. There are a few basic rules which will be given later on how this can be done, but the solution is largely dependent on your own sensitivity. You should study the works of others and, by analyzing successful compositions, you will discover reliable guideposts. Work away with your sketch book. Try variations on one theme and gradually you will "feel" what is right and what is wrong. It is not simply a question of shape and mass, light and shade, tone and color; *all* these features must be considered. A picture should not give a feeling of being unbalanced; therefore, you must weigh accent against accent, richness against richness, so that the finished painting will give the viewer a feeling of harmony and balance, the sense of satisfaction which most certainly you experienced in creating it.

Of the various subjects which you might paint, few give the same challenge or excitement as a landscape or seascape. In a landscape, the question of selection is extremely important. The range of possible subject matter is much wider than in a still life or a portrait. You must decide exactly what part of the scene you will place in your particular rectangle.

Fig. 6. Finding your picture in a landscape

Look at Fig. 6. This is a view of a rock formation known as the Needles, which juts out into the sea off the Isle of Wight, near England. The dotted line, the "frame," indicates a pleasing arrangement for a painting of this subject. The three pine trees with their tall trunks give a needed vertical note in the foreground to counteract the strong line of the rock formation of the Needles themselves, streaming out to the right of the picture, and to the horizontal lines of the field, the fence and the skyline. In this particular picture, the houses and cottages to the left would not add importance to the scene. Rather, they would inevitably detract from the principal component, the rock formation. However one placed them on the canvas, they would be in the left-hand corner and thus draw the eye away from the center of the picture. The path going to the gate helps to lead the eye through the gate and into the picture. The trunks of the trees act not only as strong verticals but also as a frame within a frame to focus the viewer's attention on the Needles themselves.

Of course, the picture could take in a great deal more of the scene. You could include the houses as well as most of the field and the path in the foreground, but doing so would not add strength. Instead, you would diminish and dwarf your main object and lose significance by the inclusion of a wide mass of green. The trees would have to be a great deal smaller and would lose their power to hold the elements of the picture together.

Perhaps the easiest way to learn how to paint a landscape is to learn what to avoid. Figs. 7-10 are four bad examples of how the scene in Fig. 6 might have been treated. Can you see what is wrong in each? In the first, the large right-hand tree has been omitted. Now the picture appears to crowd toward the left, while the long line of the Needles has nothing to check it on the right. The path has been moved to the left, too. This serves to emphasize the crowding effect in that corner of the picture, and it does not lead into the scene as well as it does in Fig. 6.

Fig. 8 shows a different lighting effect. The sun has previously

Fig. 7. Omission of right-hand tree

Fig. 8. Cutting up of a mass, omission of trees and fence, different lighting

Fig. 9. Omission of left-hand trees

Fig. 10. Skyline too high

Examples showing weakness in composition in dealing with the scene in Fig. 6

been behind the cliffs, thus throwing the Needles into shadow and relief against the light tones of the sea. Now the sun shines directly on the white chalk cliffs, which lose strength and tone value as a result. Fig. 8 is far less dramatic than Fig. 6.

The removal of the trees emphasizes the need for something to balance the horizontal and vertical features in a picture of this nature. In this version the main features—the horizon, the line of the cliffs, the line of the woods and the line of the field—are all straight horizontals, and add up to an unsatisfactory composition.

The cloud in the top right-hand corner points to another mistake, that is, the cutting up of a principal shape by the edge of the frame. Quite obviously, the picture cannot be endless. You must give it a boundary, but you must watch with great care how you place it. The single cloud—which in itself, if placed correctly in the sky, would be quite satisfactory—here produces a very poor effect because it is cut in half at the border. Notice, too, that the removal of the fence, the track and the little shrubs weakens the foreground. There is nothing to lead the eye into the picture and there is no point of interest for it to rest on before proceeding to the Needles themselves.

The third example (Fig. 9), again is lighted from the front; the cliffs thus lose power. In addition, the line of the woods has been dropped. They have become an insignificant fringe, almost a hedge, rather than a dark silhouette as a foreground for the sea and rocks beyond. Restoring even one tree does help, but its placing is bad. It partly obscures the Needles, and so makes the picture largely pointless, as its principal feature has become confused, if not completely obscured.

The next illustration (Fig. 10) illustrates a glaringly bad horizon line. To achieve your effect of being either high up or low down in relation to a picture, the placing of the horizon is important. To achieve the effect of being on the beach you must bring the line well down. On the other hand, if you are on a high, lofty hill, as in this picture, the horizon line needs to be brought well up. But this is too far! When the horizon is only an inch or two below the top of the frame, anything represented in the sky will be so small that it will have no importance. It will not "read," that is, be recognizable for the viewer. Making all your components in a picture clear, making it possible for the viewer to understand them, is a factor you must watch for in every part of the painting. However well drawn, an object that is partly obscured or badly lighted can easily lose its meaning as well as its role in the composition of the picture.

Fig. 11 briefly shows how this picture might have been painted had the rectangle been vertical rather than horizontal. The vertical canvas rarely succeeds for a landscape, although you might occasionally use it for a picture of a tree or group of trees, or of some houses in a street scene. The example here shows that

Fig. 11. Up-and-down picture looks cut down

however you twist it around, a vertical frame will inevitably make the picture appear cut down. This does not result in a harmonious rendering of the subject. The fact that the Needles are given great prominence does not necessarily point to their having great pictorial importance; in fact, by the omission of the main mass of the cliff and the two other trees, the Needles are actually weakened. The placing of the gate and path gives an inescapable feeling that the picture has slipped to the left.

How can you be certain of success with a landscape composition? As has already been mentioned, experience is the finest teacher; but by following the simple points that are mentioned here, you can avoid much of the awkwardness typical of an amateur.

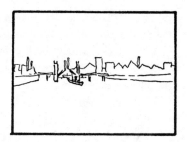

Fig. 12. Overcrowding   Fig. 13. Dwarfing

Figs. 12 and 13 illustrate two common faults of beginners. The scene is on the busy English river, the Thames, and in Fig. 12 the artist has been working too close to his subject. He has framed the principal objects awkwardly. The right-hand leaf of the drawbridge juts awkwardly through the border of the frame, and the forecastle and smokestack of the ship underneath are unsatisfactory. Notice how confusion arises due to awkward placing: the mast of the ship in the foreground is too close to the mast of the ship in the background, and both of them line up with the badly placed chimneys in the distance. This haphazard placing of the principal shapes causes overcrowding. To avoid this, use your sketch book. Try several different compositions before you begin the picture. A few quick notes and a few bare lines will help you avoid errors in composition.

Fig. 13 is the antithesis of Fig. 12. Here, the artist is *too far away* from his subject. However, proper distance is not necessarily a question of *where* you stand or sit to paint; what matters is the impression of distance you give on your canvas. This particular composition might have been successful with an alternative feature or point of interest, such as a tug and a stream of barges, or some ships or yachts at anchor in the foreground, to give the eye something to rest on and bring it into the picture. But as it is, you have only a wide expanse of water with nothing to lead your eye toward the objects in the background. The distant bank, although it recedes, is too far away, and in the far distance it is confused by what must necessarily be a complicated collection of objects—the ship, the raised arms of the bridge, its towers, the chimneys and the docks beyond.

Here again the question of selection is vital. One method of solving it is to hold up your two hands, the fingers upward and the two thumbs joined horizontally. This will give you a make-shift frame, and you can swing your hands around at different distances from your eyes to help you find the best possible rectangle for your picture. A more efficient method is to cut out a rectangle of the same proportion as your picture from cardboard, and use it in a similar manner. You will find this device very useful until you have trained your eye to see the picture automatically.

Figs. 14-16 are examples of compositional difficulties and their solutions. In Fig. 14 (left), symmetry is shown, that is, the exact

Fig. 14. Symmetry   Altered viewpoint

balancing of one object by another, often around a centrally placed focal point. Symmetry may well have its place in design or poster work where strong emphasis is needed, but for the noncommercial artist symmetry tends to produce overemphasis and at the same time dullness and monotony in the picture. Now look at the placing of the monument and the two churches in Fig.

14 (right). See how asymmetry at once increases the harmony of the composition. The mere moving of the monument so that it groups up with the church on the left produces interest and also gives an added importance to the second church, which is now relatively isolated on the right.

Study the use of symmetry and asymmetry by looking at the works of the great painters of the past and of today. You will find very few examples of symmetry except in portraits or still lifes. Even in these, although the figure or principal object may be placed centrally, its symmetrical position will usually be offset by the careful use of light and shade.

The two examples in Fig. 15 illustrate another mistake—having a central line, either horizontal or vertical, exactly dividing the canvas or picture. In the drawing on the left the skyline and the trunk of a tree produce an unsatisfactory composition. The tree stops the eye and prevents it from moving into the picture, while the centrally placed skyline gives the composition a feeling of unsatisfactory balance. When you move the trunk to one side and lower the skyline, as in the sketch on the right, you improve the composition.

Fig. 15. Central placing   Off center and lower skyline

In Fig. 16 are two examples of a flower painting, always a popular type of picture. A flower itself has such beauty and grace,

Fig. 16. An elaborate background
loses the flowers

Plain background, but picture
should be up and down

not only of shape but also of color, that in most cases it is quite
satisfactory to place it against a plain background. If you do use a
background pattern, avoid what happened in the example on the
left. Here, a particularly strong design in the backcloth conflicts
with the blooms themselves. The flowers are lost against the design. It would have probably been better to use a pattern in the
cloth or the ground on which the vase or pot is standing, as in the
example on the right. The flower is much more dramatic against
the plain backcloth, although, as the dotted line indicates, it
would have been still better in a vertical canvas.

The composition of a still life is fascinating and gives you scope
for endless imagination. The early Dutch masters of this type of
picture showed amazing technical ability. Their glass, pewter,
fruit, bunches of grapes, peeled oranges and similar subjects were
depicted with great skill. So complete was their command over
light and shade that, despite photographic exactness, their
paintings glow with life and reality.

Chardin, a French painter of the eighteenth century, was one of
the greatest masters of still life, and showed us hidden beauties in
the simplest of everyday articles: reflections in a glass of water,
beautiful soft tones in the bloom on fresh plums. Gustave Courbet
was another Frenchman working in the nineteenth century. He

liked to turn his hand from stormy landscapes to studies of small bowls of fruit, two or three apples, a couple of pears, working at them with the visionary eye of a true artist to show that even in the simplest of objects there is a great beauty. Even today many painters still work with still lifes.

In making a still life you can draw upon almost anything: for example, mushrooms of different sizes and of different ages will produce a tremendous variety of soft browns and grays and pinks, and you can achieve variety in shapes if some are upside-down and some are on their side and some are facing toward you, with their little radial fins and cream tops. A fresh fish, if placed on a sympathetic background and lighted carefully, produces a wonderful display of color—the bright red of the gills and the pale belly shining with blues, creams and sea greens.

One advantage of the still life is that you can control your model. Unlike a landscape, once you have set it and have lighted it in the particular way you want, it will remain static. You can concentrate entirely on getting your tone values correct.

Painters often talk of tone, and you will find this one of the most important factors when working on a picture. Tone is the depth of a particular color. Many teachers say, "It doesn't matter about having your color exact. It's far more important to have your tones correct." This is perfectly true, for a picture will be harmonious regardless of the colors chosen if the various tones of the colors are correct. To get your tones in the right relationships, look at two colors next to each other and be guided by their comparative depths of color.

Perhaps you have heard—and wondered about—the term "artist's license." This may be a difficult phrase to understand completely, and it is one that has been greatly misunderstood at different times. Selection is a factor which has a good deal to do with license. When you look at a subject which you feel has the makings of a picture, take your sketch book and gradually rough it into a form of composition that satisfies you. In so doing, you may feel that various parts of the view are not necessary and can be omitted. You may also want to move some parts to obtain the desired composition. When you do this, do not think that you are "cheating." It is the final result by which you will be judged. In composition or in painting use whatever method you feel will be most satisfactory.

Fig. 17 shows a scene which you might easily come across in the country: a little farmyard cluttered with telephone wires, a telegraph pole, old tin cans, and a large billboard on the left beside the house. Perhaps you may feel that it makes a very reasonable composition as it stands. But another painter might find that for him it is altogether too cluttered. Fig. 18 is a thumbnail sketch of the scene reduced to its essentials. The artist has taken a little license with it. He decided, for example, to open the gate so that the eye can pass more easily to the rest of the picture. He also noticed that behind the billboard was a view of a

Fig. 17

Fig. 18. Simplification and selection
This sketch shows the principal shapes of the scene opposite reduced to its
basic essentials.

tiny village, so he omitted the billboard. The eye, traveling
through the gate, past the house and field, eventually reaches the
village. This is an example of recession. Do you feel the telegraph
poles and the wires are really necessary? There is a strong vertical
and an equally strong horizontal, but do these lines really add to
the composition? These are questions you should ask yourself in
planning the composition of any picture.

Double and even triple recession was very popular with the
Dutch painters of interiors. They liked to lead the viewer down
passages and through room after room. Recession is also typical of
Dutch landscapes. Hobbema in "The Avenue, Middelharnis"
(see Plate 1 on page 32), with its long avenue stretching away
into the distance, cleverly illustrates this technique. On one side
is a gardener pruning some trees, and at different intervals down

Plate I. "The Avenue, Middelharnis" by Meindert Hobbema (1638-1709)

the road are little groups of figures. As your eye goes past one group and then another, on past a cluster of houses, and still farther into the picture, you have a sense of unending space.

To return to Figs. 17 and 18, you must remember when sketching a complicated scene like this small farmyard, first to reduce it to its basic shapes. This was done in Fig. 18. Don't worry about detail. Just place your lines as broadly as you possibly can. Incidentally, when drawing houses, do open one or two windows. This gives a greater feeling of reality than if they are all shown sealed. How you represent the rest of the objects—the chickens, the line of washing, the cans—is up to you. In most cases, a simple treatment results in a more forceful picture.

When choosing a subject for a landscape or a seascape, don't

32

just sit down in front of the first pretty view you come to; very seldom will this make a successful picture. First, walk around, examine the scene from different angles, use your cardboard frame, make a sketch. Eventually you find an arrangement of shapes or masses which will satisfy you.

In Fig. 19 a number of mistakes have been made deliberately. How many can you recognize? First, the stark lifeboat station is placed almost centrally in the picture, which accentuates its huge, unrelieved concrete wall. You could correct this fault by using your imagination. For example, you might place some boats on the beach, their masts leaning against the wall of the lifeboat station, or you could paint the concrete as though it were chipped away, here and there showing the red bricks underneath. A second flaw is that the steps, undoubtedly one of the most interesting parts of the actual scene, were squeezed into the right-

Fig. 19. A picture that breaks nearly all the rules

hand side of the picture. The tall, dark object on the extreme right is not clear enough to be recognized. It was actually an old lamp-post, certainly a shape too interesting to cut away with the edge of the frame.

Notice, also, the poor treatment of the chimneys. Some do not even have a roof to stand on. Although the viewer will undoubtedly assume there are roofs underneath, it is not wise to show them in such a vague manner. Furthermore, if the smoke from these chimneys were blowing toward the left, it would have helped to draw the composition together. Blowing to the right, however, the smoke only emphasizes the picture's general lack of balance.

Now, notice the placement of the yacht. It seems to pull the elements of the picture toward the left; this is because it is in full sail and very near the left boundary line. Not only that, the direction of its sails and pennant illustrates the very elementary mistake of showing the wind blowing in two directions at once! Points like these may seem obvious, but in the heat of the moment, and perhaps when you are working with a crowd of onlookers breathing down your neck, you can easily err!

When you turn to pictures you can paint indoors, the difficulty of composition is somewhat lessened, for you don't have to select your subject from such a wide scene. Of course, you will still have to solve problems of balance and arrangement. Flower painting in particular requires forethought in arranging the model, as well as in transforming it on the canvas. Lighting, which will be dealt with more fully in the following chapter, is also of great importance, for by the careful use of well-directed light you can bring your model to life and make the most of reflected lights and colors.

The illustrations in Fig. 20 give you some pointers on setting up flower arrangements. They show two different ways of placing some lilies growing in a flowerpot. In the one on the left, the model has been deliberately placed to the right to avoid a dull symmetry, but this leaves too much blank space on the left. One possible

Fig. 20. Too far to the right
Balanced by the inclusion of a second plant

solution is the introduction of a second plant, as in the picture on the right. However, the added plant should be quite small, so as not to detract from the magnificence of the lilies.

A bowl of roses is one of the most beautiful flower pieces you can paint. It is full of deep, rich color, but be careful: it requires special treatment. To achieve harmony on the canvas, you must exert great care not only in the placing of the bowl of flowers but also in arranging the blossoms so that they fall into some simple pattern. A raggle-taggle effect such as that shown in Fig. 21A (top) may appear lively, but it is seldom harmonious when framed. In Fig. 21A (bottom) the roses, the leaves and the bottom of the bowl have been brought into a basic oval shape. This is one way to fit them into the frame in a harmonious manner.

Over-ragged composition, badly placed

Fig. 21A.

An apparently careless arrangement actually conforms to a basic shape

The examples in Fig. 21B illustrate the difference between a cluttered and a simple arrangement. Fig. 21B (left) shows a bowl of flowers by itself, well arranged, well lighted against a suitable background and on a suitable base. On the right, you have the same bowl of flowers and the same background, but various other objects have been introduced into the picture. One or two of them might have made it more interesting, but certainly a crowd of new objects makes the composition fussy and reduces its strength as a whole.

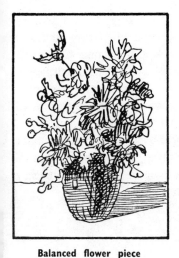

Balanced flower piece

Fig. 21B.

Confusion and loss of strength caused by inserting articles unrelated to the main subject

Resist the temptation to pile model upon model. It is a mistake to think that this will show off your painting ability. Many a beautiful flower study or landscape has been wrecked by the laying on of detail and putting in of unnecessary objects. Whatever you put into your painting, whether in a seascape or a flower piece, ask yourself if it is really necessary. You can test by making a preliminary sketch of the objects you intend to group together.

Again turn to the works of the great painters and observe how, through simplicity, they achieve brilliant effects. The French Impressionists were particularly good at this. They placed on their canvases only what was necessary to bring a picture to life. With his simple, quiet landscapes Alfred Sisley achieves far more than many Victorian artists who included every last twig and tiny leaf. Sisley and his contemporary, Pissarro, stroked in their color and their tones, absolutely true, and thereby conveyed the image to the eye of the viewer.

John Constable and Joseph Turner, working about a century before the Impressionists, started this trend away from academic exactness. If you have the chance to look at an original Constable, stand up close and notice how the artist has put in his principal shapes—for example, towering, majestic trees. They are painted on a dark red ochre canvas with the broadest possible treatment, lights stippled on and brushed in with tremendous vigor. Then, slowly retreat and in an almost magical way, when you are about six or seven paces away from the painting, it will appear that he actually painted every leaf and every twig. This evoked imagery is one of the greatest heights to which painting can rise.

III

PERSPECTIVE AND SHADOW

The artists of Egypt and Greece, painting two thousand years ago, composed and carried out their work with little feeling for perspective or the correct use of shadows. This was also true of the painters of Europe up to the fourteenth century. Although the ancient Romans employed perspective, the art was lost and not rediscovered until the fourteenth and fifteenth centuries. It is interesting to study the earlier masters and follow their struggles to impart this feeling of recession. Often they placed their vanishing points incorrectly or used too many of them, which sometimes gave their pictures an odd appearance of distortion.

If you study a painting from an Egyptian tomb or temple, you will see that everything is shown either in profile or as a flat shape, having just two dimensions, and with no attempt to give it a feeling of growing smaller as it recedes from the viewer. A painting which does not embody perspective, the name given to the principles which govern this recession of objects and planes, will always appear unnatural. If you look at the sketches of a child of three or four years of age, all the objects will appear to be vertical. If the picture shows a flat field, you will have no sense of recession but will seem to look straight down on it. Even if there are figures or objects such as tractors or farm buildings in the picture, you will still get the feeling of a map or diagram, rather than a picture.

In the paintings of professional artists the use of color and shadow and of perspective gives a feeling of recession or depth. Perspective in particular can be extremely complicated, but it is not necessary or even advisable for the beginning painter to go into the finer points or the elaborate geometric projections used by some artists. However, you should understand the essentials of perspective.

In Fig. 22 (left), the church appears flat, drawn without perspective. It has only two dimensions, height and width, and there is no indication of the construction of the building. Since it

Fig. 22. A simple building without and with perspective

is of a uniform width, the path leading away from the church door does not seem to approach the viewer. When the same building is viewed in perspective, as in Fig. 22 (right), you can at once perceive a third dimension; you get an impression of the width of the building and also of how it is constructed. You see how the roof joins the tower, and that the wall of the chancel is set back slightly from the base of the tower. The path really seems to come toward you.

You can achieve perspective in several ways, all of which employ what are called vanishing points or invisible dots toward which all the horizontal lines in the picture will appear to converge.

Fig. 23 demonstrates the use of a single vanishing point. The sketch is of a market garden, and the small black cross at a point

Fig. 23. Single vanishing point

approximately centered in the picture represents the single invisible vanishing point. If traced out, the lines of the vegetable patch, the horizontal lines of the greenhouse and of the houses themselves, would all reach this point. Notice how this use of perspective gives a feeling of depth to the picture. You can find such points in nature if you know what to look for. For example, if you stand on a football field at one goal post and look toward the opposite end, you will see how the boundary lines of the field and the seats in the grandstand tend to converge.

Although you can use a single vanishing point in a landscape, a more satisfactory method employs two such points. In Fig. 24 the ground line represents the front or lower edge of the picture, and the skyline is at the eye level of the average person. Your vanishing point should be along the eye level line. When an architect produces plans for buildings, he has to set up elaborate projections and he arrives geometrically at these two points. But it is

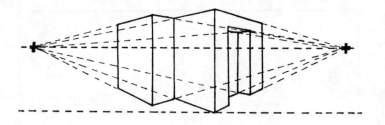

Fig. 24. Setting up a perspective
The bottom dotted line is the ground line and the upper dotted line represents the eye level, along which the vanishing points lie.

not necessary for you to use such complicated means. Place the two points at a convenient distance on either side of your drawing at the eye level line. Now, all you have to do when planning your drawing is extend or produce all your planes facing right to the right-hand point, and vice versa with the planes facing left.

Fig. 25 demonstrates three different uses of the double vanishing point. In each the crane, the crate and the building in the background are given a definite organization through this treatment. The top drawing treats the scene in what is called "worm's-eye" perspective, meaning that the eye level and the vanishing points are dropped down to ground level. This gives the viewer a feeling of looking up and can be used very dramatically if you are drawing or painting large buildings. Now, look at the bottom sketch. If you wish to give a feeling of being in an airplane, or being on the top of a high cliff looking down, raise the eye level and vanishing points as far as you feel is effective. This gives the viewer the feeling of looking down at the scene. The center drawing places the vanishing point at eye level as in Fig. 24.

An example of perspective in an interior, Fig. 26, shows that the easiest plan is again to use just one point to produce your horizontal lines. You can alter the perceived shape of the room

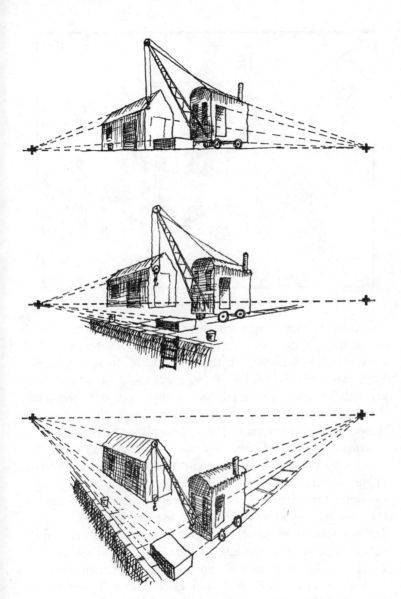

Fig. 25. Worm's-eye, normal and bird's-eye perspective

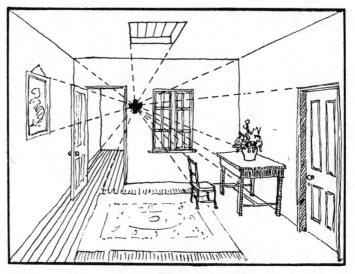

Fig. 26. Interior perspective

by sliding the vanishing point along the eye level. In this sketch the centrally placed point gives a square view of the room. The more you slide it to the left, the right side of the room becomes more noticeable. Of course, if you move the point to the right, you will automatically emphasize the left portion of the room. Remember that *every* object in your painting must be drawn in perspective, the verticals to the vertical plane, horizontals to the horizontal. This is an important rule. Nothing looks worse than a row of houses in which the windows and doorways are tipped out of the vertical. In the case of an interior sketch, not only must the walls, the doorway and the pictures recede, but also the rug, the table and any other furniture in the room.

Obviously, when you are out sketching, it is not necessary to set up these vanishing points on your paper or canvas. In many cases it would be impossible to do so because they would fall somewhere in space beyond your easel. You will save yourself much time and effort by practicing before you actually paint.

Practice on some *large* sheets of paper rather than in your sketch book, so that you will have room to place your vanishing points on the paper and to get the feel of producing your lines in correct relation to them. Soon you will find that the use of perspective becomes almost automatic. You will *sense* these planes.

A problem that you will come across in perspective, especially in landscape, is how to make a road go uphill or downhill. Fig. 27 gives two views, one up, the other downhill. To achieve either effect, alter the vanishing point of the road. If you want to make the street go uphill, bring the vanishing point for the road above the horizon or eye level line. To make your street go downhill, drop the point onto which the two sides of the road converge, leaving the vanishing point for the rest of your buildings on the horizon or eye level. By alternating the positions of your vanishing points you can suggest different gradients and, if you move the point from side to side in the picture, you can indicate a turn in the road. The techniques described here will work for flights of stairs, too.

Early mastery of these basic rules is of great importance. If you do not use them correctly, your drawings of buildings or ships or

Fig. 27. Uphill and downhill perspective—the horizontal dotted line shows the eye level.

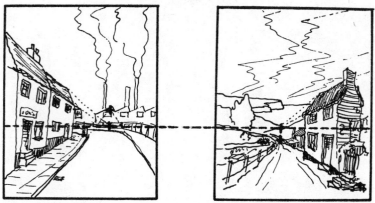

any solid objects will appear distorted. No matter how beautifully painted, your picture will be a disappointment.

SHADOW

The placement of shadows in a picture is just as important as perspective. It, too, can be a very complicated matter if it is worked out geometrically. But for most artists, particularly beginners, careful observation and planning are sufficient.

Before you start a picture, always notice where your light is coming from. All too often the beginner charges into his subject, and then, in the last few moments, tries hastily to put in a few shadows to indicate his source of light. Look at the simple sketches of a poplar tree in Fig. 28. In the left sketch the light is coming from the right. You can see how the right-hand side of the tree is lighted up, while the left-hand side is dark. The tree casts a long, oval shadow. In the other drawing the light is from directly over-head. Thus, the whole shape of the tree seems different. Now it is dark around the base and stands in a small round pool of shade.

In a picture which has a great many features—trees, buildings, people, bridges and other objects—the direction of the light

Fig. 28. Light direction

influences the whole aspect of the picture. Therefore, firmly fix in your mind where your light is coming from before you start even the simplest painting. Think of the direction of the light. At the same time, think of light as something which is splashing across your picture, illuminating the near sides of everything in its path, and casting the far sides into shadow.

Light is also essential to bring out the modeling in the objects you are painting. Teach yourself to observe what happens in nature. Light gives not only shape, but also color, and produces infinite subtleties which you must train your eye to see. For example, take a simple cooking pot, and place it so that it is well lighted from one side. In Fig. 29 there is a group of still life objects lighted from the left. Notice how the light strikes the pot, highlighting it on the left. Next is an area of halftone, merging into deep shadow and, finally a light strip, caused by illumination having crept around the saucepan. There is a feeling of a little soft half-light down the right side of the round objects which you can also see on the saucepan, on the jug and on the oranges. The correct indication of highlight, halftone, deep shadow and above all reflected light is what gives body to any drawn or painted object. Try it and see. Draw a pot quite quickly, using shadows but leaving out the reflected light on the right side. Notice how this omission robs the subject of its natural roundness.

At first color in the shadows presents quite a problem. The temptation is just to make a shadow dark—brown or even black. But such a treatment will not give a feeling of depth. Your eye should be able to penetrate the shadows, to go around the saucepan, in between the box and the fruit shown in Fig. 29.

Many of the greatest paintings owe part of their fascination to the handling of light. The French Impressionists were not only revolutionary in their treatment of color and composition, but they also deliberately exploited light and shade. Many of their pictures are painted with the figures or the most important parts in shadow. You can see how they treated the flesh tones in shade

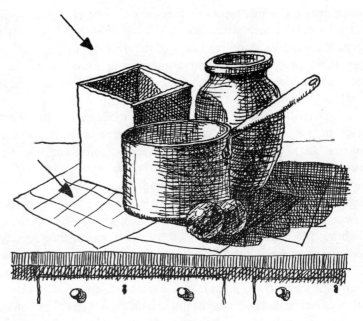

Fig. 29. Shadows cast

and how they brought out the warmth of shadows cast by a strong midday sun. Many other painters, too, were masters of shade and shadow. One of these was Caravaggio, an Italian. For example, in "The Supper at Emmaus," (see Plate 2) he used light so dramatically that the full force of the highlight is concentrated on Jesus, bringing the viewer's eye straight to the focal point of the picture. If you try to imagine different ways of lighting the subject—from the front, from above or even with a secondary light to one side— you will be able to visualize how the use of lighting can completely alter any composition. Another painter who was extremely fond of dramatic lighting effects was Rembrandt. In nearly all of his pictures he uses a restricted source of light, yet in his shadows there is a tremendous suggestion of depth and of atmosphere.

Plate 2. "The Supper at Emmaus" by Caravaggio (1573-1610)

The sketches in Fig. 30 illustrate very briefly the importance of light and shade in a landscape. In the top example the pier is recognizable as such, but it has no feeling of depth or shape. In the second example a few simply sketched shadows have been added; the feeling of space under the pier, the shape of the buildings, the dome and the ship are accentuated at once. Many a composition whose components are appealing can be improved still further by a skillful application of light and shade. Sometimes symmetry can be offset by the placing of shadows. Often, you can make vague or partially drawn shapes comprehensible to the viewer by the shadows which they cast upon other objects or upon the ground.

Many teachers insist that the only correct position for the source of light is 45 degrees, either left or right. For many years

49

Fig. 30. The effect of shadows

this was an academic dictum, but today it is by no means considered unbreakable. Constable was one of the first to break with it. He liked to paint with the sun directly overhead, causing pools of deep, luminous shadow to fall around the bases of his trees, around his figures, and deep shadows to form under the eaves of the buildings and under the sills of the window. At other times, he painted early morning or late evening scenes with the sun low in the sky, so that light streamed across his landscapes horizontally, casting large dark, dramatic shapes over the fields. Turner, another great innovator, lighted his scenes from all points of the compass. Often it is difficult to decide where his light source is; the pictures almost seem to generate light themselves.

PERSPECTIVE THROUGH TONE AND COLOR

Perspective and shadow are of paramount importance to give a feeling of recession and depth to your picture, and to give substance to the objects you paint. But there is also a third technique

50

which you should study: tone and color control. In a landscape, the colors in the foreground seem stronger in tone and brighter in hue than those in the background. All colors tend to become more blue as they disappear toward the horizon, perhaps in softly undulating fields or distant hills.

In landscape painting, it is very important to work on your picture as a whole. That is, do not attempt to finish any one part first, and do not try to put in your brightest or your darkest colors or tones right away. To start with, paint as though your hands were playing a melody in the center of the keyboard of a piano. Then, as the picture slowly takes shape, you can become more dramatic and place your dark tones and your sparkling highlights in exactly the right places. If you do this too early, you may find as you get near the end of your picture that you have nothing left in power or strength on your palette with which to put on the last few finishing touches.

The control of color is quite evident in the work of such painters as Pissarro and Sisley, but you can also see many fine examples in current exhibitions. All good painters use highlights and shadows carefully. Strangely enough, the use of pure black or white does not necessarily add that final sparkle or that last, strong, dark note. On the contrary, it will often give an artificial feeling to the picture as a whole. In fact, black is a color which is difficult to use effectively. As a beginner, you should avoid it. Pure black seldom appears in nature. It is always picking up a reflection from something near it—for example, a green bush. Even a black painted object hardly ever appears as plain black.

Picking out the colors in shadows requires keen observation. It is comparatively easy to pick the right tone or hue for the sky, or the brightly lighted foreground of a field, or for the red brick of a house. But it is much more difficult to select the right colors for tree trunks or for water in a small stream. Water, itself colorless, takes on various shades from objects around it. By looking into the bed of a stream, you may be able to discover what has given the water its particular color. Sometimes, for example, it is reddish-brown sediment washed down by a heavy rain. In a clear stream, brown stones or weeds on the bed or the bank will impart their color to the water. If you paint a stream from a distance, its color will depend on those of the trees and bushes reflected in it. Of course the sea takes on the general tone of the sky. The farther you are from a body of water, the more it will seem to provide a mirror for whatever is above it.

In working from nature avoid painting hard lines around your various subjects. If you outline a bush, tree or building with a strong dark-toned line, you tend to destroy the illusion of perspective and give the object the appearance of a piece of scenery cut out and standing on a stage. Generally speaking, nothing in nature has hard outlines. The picture should be soft in its outlines, achieving its shape from your use of light and shade; the subtle introduction of a reflected light can do more than anything else to give the viewer the feeling that what he sees before him has an anatomy of its own. He senses its roundness and feels that he could walk around it (a tree or post, for example), because it appears to stand in an atmosphere of its own.

Before starting a picture you may become discouraged by the mass of intricate details in front of you. You just do not know where to start. The solution is very simple: Try to visualize your picture broadly, as a series of shapes, receding one behind the other. When he looks at his model, a person, a seascape, or a collection of buildings, the painter must reduce it to the simplest possible basic shapes. You, too, can do this by half closing your eyes. Try it; you will find that the fussy details have vanished, the lighting becomes simplified and you easily perceive the plain masses of the scene. Draw these first. Get them onto your canvas or piece of paper, and you will be surprised how many difficulties have been removed. You will have the skeleton of the plain masses to build on. Later, you can fill in as much or as little detail as you like.

IV

YOUR MATERIALS

COLORS

Today's artist can choose from a wide variety of bright and rich colors, compared with those available four hundred years ago during the great era of painting of the Italian Renaissance. You can buy hundreds of different colors. Some of the pigments described here are synthetic, that is, artificially produced, but others are natural substances which have been used since the prehistoric beginnings of painting.

Colors are unquestionably the most important item in the artist's list of materials. Take care in their selection, and buy only those sold by reputable manufacturers.

The *Yellows* include cadmium yellow, a very strong bright tint, which will keep its power even when diluted with a large quantity of white. Yellow ochre is an earth color, rather dull, but extremely useful for mixing with other shades. Sometimes, too, you will want to use it by itself.

Reds: cadmium, like the yellow, is very strong, bright and clean. Indian red, another natural color, produces pleasing tones in brickwork and also, when used with a blue and a yellow, will give a beautiful soft gray. Alizarin crimson, an artificial color coming from coal, is useful for glazing where transparency is needed. It can produce a subtle range of pinks when mixed with white.

Most of the *Blues* are quite safe to use. Cobalt is a gentle color, more suitable for water color than oils. Ultramarine, a strong, rich pigment, today takes the place of the real ultramarine, which came from the semi-precious stone lapis lazuli. Cerulean, introduced during the last century, is a very pleasant pale blue with a slight green tinge which can be successfully used with sky tones and also intermixed with other colors. Prussian blue is an immensely strong pigment. This is one of the most powerful tinting colors available to the artist. Use it with discretion, for even a tiny portion will more than stand up to ten times the amount of many of the other colors in a mixture.

The *Greens* include cadmium, which has the same characteristics as the other cadmium colors. Viridian is a clear, cool, transparent blue-green. Oxide of chromium is an opaque, strong, pleasant, warm tint. Many greens such as sap and olive (Hooker's) are unstable in most media.

The *Browns* have not altered materially for the past two thousand years: siennas and umbers, both burnt and raw. In both cases the raw tints are the cooler, while the burnt ones produce warm, strong tones.

Blacks are normally quite safe, whether ivory, lamp, peach or vine. Ivory used by itself in oils is liable to crack, but you can prevent this by mixing a small amount of some more stable pigment with it in order to avoid danger of future disfigurement.

Of the *Whites*, the old favorite flake, or lead white, is still as popular as it was centuries ago. It is a fine coverer. Zinc white has a beautiful bluish tinge, covers well, and is extremely fluid. Titanium white, the latest developed, is probably the best, being both non-poisonous and also extremely opaque. It is a fine covering pigment.

The basic pigments are the same in the various media. Cadmium yellow pigment, for example, is identical in water color with the pigment used in a cadmium yellow oil, pastel or poster color.

Water color contains the basic pigments ground in water. It is then mixed with various gums and other substances to provide a different consistency for each of the three forms available, cake, stick or tube.

Oil colors are ground straight into oil. Poster colors are ground into gum. Tempera, which was a great favorite with many of the earlier painters, is becoming increasingly popular today. It is probably the most permanent method of painting known. The colors are ground in egg yolk. However, today a type of tempera is available which eliminates the messiness of mixing in egg.

Fresco painting is an interesting but little-known medium in which the artist applies the color directly to damp plaster, working alongside the plasterer. This is how the great Italian Michelangelo worked his wonderful ceiling of the Sistine Chapel in Rome. Fresco calls for considerable control and directness of approach. It should not be attempted except by an absolute master.

Encaustic is another medium in which the color is applied with hot wax. It was very popular with the early Greeks and Egyptians and is enjoying a modest vogue today.

During the centuries many artists have concerned themselves practically and in theory with ideas and scientific treatises on color, how it should be used, and how colors react in various treatments. Colors are basically divided into three that are termed primary: red, blue and yellow. Intermixing the primary colors produces the secondaries: orange, green and purple.

Fig. 31 is a color circle which includes the primary and secondary tints as well as the intermediaries. It is very useful and will

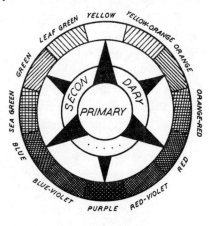

Fig. 31. The color circle

55

provide a ready guide when "cool" and "warm" colors are mentioned: those on the blue side of the circle are said to be cool while those on the opposite side are warm. Colors which are opposite each other in the color wheel are called complementary colors. Many painters have worked with these complementaries, notably the French Impressionists and the later Post-Impressionists. An artist employing this method places two complementary colors together to produce the maximum effect from both. For instance, yellow and purple or red and green will produce the strongest effect when used in combination. This is called complementary harmony.

The color wheel can also be used to produce a second form of color harmony called analogous. This means that when three colors next to each other on the wheel are placed together in a picture, they will produce an effect of concord rather than discord. Blue, green-blue, and green are a good example of analogous harmony.

You can also paint in monochrome. This simply means using different tones of one color. Dark brown, for example, when inter-mixed with varying degrees of white, will produce a vast range of tints.

BRUSHES

After buying colors you will have to select some brushes. The water-colorist ordinarily will use a soft hair brush. The best of these are made from Kolinsky sable and can, in the very finest grades, be extremely expensive. However, a good sable brush is a wonderful tool, utterly reliable. It will last a lifetime. Cheaper grades of sable are available as are coarser hairs such as ring cat, pony and ox ear. The brush shapes available are shown in Plate 3, and include the round, which is self-descriptive; the flat, which may be up to an inch wide, with hairs about three-quarters to one inch long; the sword, which is the one on the right of the group in this illustration, and which is shaped so as to provide a head that will draw a long, crisp line with considerable control; and

Plate 3. Water-color brushes

lastly, for the water-colorist, a mop. This is a large rather floppy-headed brush meant solely for applying areas of wash. If you wish, you may buy brushes already packaged in sets.

The oil painter, too, has several shapes from which to choose. His brushes should be made of a fine white bristle; as his color is stiff, the softer brushes used in water coloring are unsuitable for controlling the paint. The brushes are round, flat and filbert, the latter being a cross between a flat and a round (Plate 4), a carefully shaped brush, which can give great delicacy of stroke. One other type can be included for oil painting where fine detail is required; that is a sable rigger, shown on the right of the group in Plate 4.

For texture painting or poster painting you can use either soft hair or bristle brushes. All shapes are suitable.

Proper care of brushes will preserve their life. Whatever your method of painting, wash them carefully at the end of each session. If oil paint hardens at the base of the bristles where they enter the metal ferrule, or if poster color clogs the soft hairs, the brushes will lose their elasticity and their color-carrying capacity, and will very soon be quite useless for painting. The water-color brush is the easiest to care for. A thorough rinsing in clean water is normally sufficient. However, the oil-painting brush needs more attention. After you have finished painting, rinse it thoroughly two or three times in turpentine and then in lukewarm water. Soak it well and scrub it around on the palm of your hand until all traces of pigment are removed. Both types of brush, after washing, should be gently reshaped with the finger tips, and left to dry in a vertical position. Besides dirt and clogging paint, both hair and bristle brushes have another enemy. The ubiquitous clothes moth dearly loves a brush, so if you are not going to use yours for a while, store it in a drawer or a box containing a little moth repellent.

OTHER MATERIALS

As far as the artist's materials are concerned, water color is a simple medium. Apart from the colors, brushes and paper, you

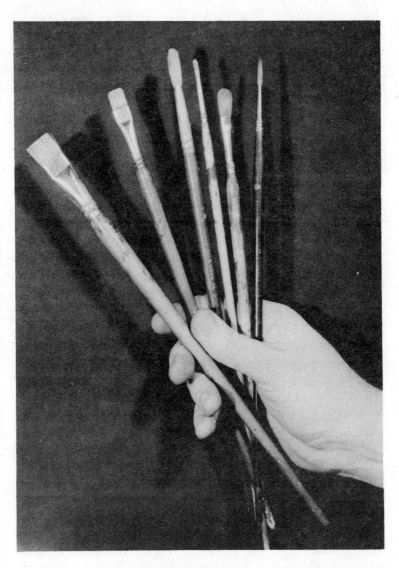

Plate 4. Oil-painting brushes

will need nothing else. But the oil painter will need a few extras to complete his outfit: at least half a pint of turpentine; a small bottle of linseed oil or copal oil medium (in case you need to dilute your color to obtain a particularly fine detail, highlight or touch); a small bottle of retouching varnish to bring up a dull patch or to provide a temporary varnish when the picture is finished. After your picture has been allowed to dry and harden for a year, you will need a final coat of clear varnish.

GROUNDS

The material you paint on is called a ground. Water colors are usually painted on paper, and you will find a variety of papers to choose from at your dealer's. The humblest of all is a rough paper which is produced from wood pulp and can be had in many different thicknesses or weights. Paper is sold in definite sizes, the most popular of which measures about 30 by 22 inches. Generally you will have to buy a whole sheet, but sometimes a good-natured dealer will cut one of these in half for you.

After the rough inexpensive papers come the handmade varieties, which undoubtedly are the best for water-color painting, as they are extremely strong, and offer a considerable choice of rough, smooth or shiny textures on which to work. These papers are all watermarked. The way to find the right side on which to work is to hold them up to the light and read the maker's name and the date of production; you should paint on the side which gives the wording from left to right.

Other papers for the water-colorist include a pleasant buff-toned, speckly, rough-textured paper. There is also a range of tinted papers (sometimes called Ingres) that can be used not only for water color but also for gouache, poster and pastel. Besides these, you will come across many other less known but perfectly reliable kinds of paper. Water-color papers as a whole are completely suitable for any form of painting other than oils. Although some artists have successfully used oils on this form of ground, it is not really an advisable practice.

If you paint in oils, your materials will be complicated and expensive. The cheapest ground is an oil-painting paper with a canvaslike texture which has been sized to reduce the degree of absorption and primed with some form of white undercoat. This is perfectly suitable for the beginner and you can obtain most of the effects of real canvas. The sheets come in pads. Before you paint stretch them, stick them down with gummed paper on a piece of cardboard, or at least pin them to a drawing board.

Somewhat more expensive are canvas boards. These are thick sheets of cardboard on which have been glued thin canvases. In many ways they resemble the final stretched canvas which most painters use. They have the same tooth and grip as a real canvas, and make excellent painting grounds.

The professional painter generally uses a real canvas tightened across a frame which is called a stretcher. The corners of the stretcher have little wedges to keep the canvas taut. You can either buy stretched canvases ready-made or make your own. This is undoubtedly the most pleasant material on which to paint, but until you are selling your works, you may find it too expensive.

Besides the grounds that you can buy, there are several that you can prepare for yourself. The simplest of these is a piece of thick cardboard. Give it a coat of sizing—diluted glue—and then two applications of white undercoat. In about a week you can paint on it. You can apply the same treatment to a piece of three-ply wood or to hardboard. Which side you use, the rough or the smooth, is a personal choice, but it is advisable to start on the smooth side. The mechanical reverse patterning on the rough side tends to absorb a great deal of color, making the application of the paint difficult.

Another ground you can prepare yourself for use with oils, water color or tempera is called a gesso panel. Gesso is a mixture of glue and plaster of Paris. This method of preparing a ground has been employed for many centuries. Most of the finest examples of early Flemish and Dutch painting are executed on this form of hard ground, which allows a very fine degree of workmanship. To prepare the gesso, dissolve two ounces of rabbitskin glue in about a pint of water in the top of a double boiler. Don't let the glue burn or boil. After it has completely dissolved, stir it into enough plaster of Paris to produce a creamy consistency. This is gesso. Then brush the gesso onto a piece of hardboard or a piece of wood and allow it to harden. Apply three or four coats. After two or three days when it is dry, sandpaper to remove any irregularities and brush-strokes. Next, if you intend to oil paint, apply a coat of sizing or shellac in an alcohol base. If it is for use with water color or tempera, leave off the final coat.

Do buy the best sketch books you can afford. They are graded from 9H, the hardest, down to 7B, which is extremely soft. To start with you might buy a 2B and a 4B or 5B. For cleaning up, a large gum eraser is very useful, as it helps to remove not only pencil but, more important, dirt, grease and other marks.

To enjoy painting to the full, especially in oils, you will want an easel. In making your selection, the principal points to look for are stability, ease of carrying and ability to hold the canvas board firmly.

These are your materials. Look after them and they will serve you well. Always put the caps back on your colors. Make sure the tubes are closed properly. As you use the color roll the tubes up from the bottom. In this way oils and water colors will last many years without hardening. An excellent plan is to have a cupboard or a drawer or, better still, a little cabinet of drawers in which to keep your materials. If you are lucky, perhaps you can find one of those small, shallow-drawered cabinets that were once used for butterfly and coin collections. Then you can have one drawer for water colors, one drawer for oils, another for brushes. If the drawers are wide enough, your paper and all your other materials can be stored away neatly and safely in the same place.

V

PAINTING IN WATER COLOR

The first people known to have painted with water colors were the ancient Egyptians. In the wonderful diagrammatic paintings in their tombs and on the walls of their temples water colors have miraculously survived the passage of time. Water color is often said to be the most difficult medium, yet this is not completely true. Even when used by a beginner its wonderful spontaneity and brightness of effect can express what the young artist is seeking.

When you buy your set of colors, you will have to choose between tubes and tins containing tablets. Stick colors are also available, but they are intended primarily for use by draftsmen and architects who wish to rub them down to make large amounts of color for washing in areas of their work. Whether you decide on pan color in a paintbox or a box or collection of tubes is a personal matter, and one on which it is hard to advise. In Plate 5 you will see tubes in use. In some ways they do have an advantage over the paintbox type, for you can squeeze an appreciable amount of color onto your palette. Thus, when painting out of doors, speedy mixing is possible. It takes a little longer when you have to stroke your tablet of color with a brush again and again to obtain the strength you wish.

The next question is the selection of colors. Usually paintboxes are ready-filled with a choice based on the advice of professional artists, and generally these boxes are entirely reliable. If you

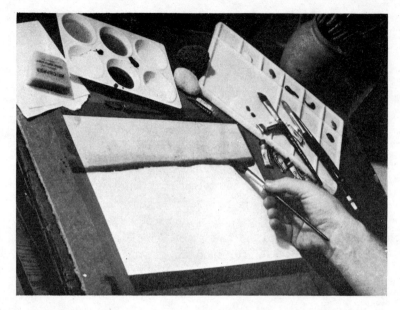

prefer, you can ask for a selection of your own choosing. This is a simple matter, especially if you are buying tubes.

Here is a list to guide you. These eleven colors should meet all your needs for working in this medium:

Cadmium yellow	Burnt umber
Yellow ochre	Ivory black
Cobalt blue	Cadmium red
Monastral blue	Indian red
Viridian	Alizarin crimson
Burnt sienna	

The brushes which you will need are shown in Plate 3. To start with, four or five will be enough: a large mop for the wash, a No. 12, a No. 8, a half-inch flat and perhaps a sword will give you all the effects you require when beginning.

As to a palette, you can of course use the lid of your specially designed paintbox or, as in Plate 5, a form of white tile with low divisions for the various colors. Another type is the white plastic with six or more wells, which holds the wash color in this picture. Saucers, plates, enameled screw caps from jars—anything of this nature will serve quite adequately.

Blotting paper is extremely useful for mopping up excess color, taking out a highlight or stopping one color from running into another if it gets out of control. Other useful accessories are a piece of clean white cotton or linen rag; a small sponge to assist in blending colors and mopping out areas; a gum eraser, a razor blade and a piece of sandpaper for tricks which will be explained later.

Before starting to paint, get to know your colors. Try out different mixtures on some odd scraps of paper. From the recommended eleven you will be able to produce literally hundreds of different tints. For instance, you can obtain a dark green from ivory black and yellow ochre. Cadmium yellow and ivory black produce another dark green.

Some of the other principal mixtures you will find useful are:

Cadmium yellow and cadmium red to produce oranges.

Cobalt and the yellows will produce greens.

You will get an intense green of tremendous power from cadmium yellow and monastral blue.

Burnt sienna and cobalt will produce a dull, dark green. Cobalt and crimson give you purple.

Ivory black will intensify both the sienna and umber. Experiment yourself, mixing one color with another in different proportions and with more or less water. Try out various brush strokes too. See what you can produce with your brushes fully loaded, moist and almost dry.

Unless you are using a very thick, heavy paper or a strong cardboard, it is an excellent plan to stretch the paper ahead of time. Lay it face downward on your drawing board or piece of hardboard on which you are going to work, and thoroughly moisten the back by means of a sponge or piece of absorbent cotton. Next, turn the paper over and repeat the process on the reverse side. As the paper expands and buckles, you have to remove the bubbles and ridges that form. Lift one end and then smooth it down again with the sponge until you have it absolutely flat. After you have gotten rid of all the irregularities, fasten the paper to the drawing board with masking tape. You will probably have to prepare your paper the day before you intend to start work; it takes about 6 hours to dry.

It is best to apply water color as lightly and directly as possible. Plate 5 shows the method for applying a flat wash such as you might need for a distant sky or a large expanse of sea. Mix your color beforehand on a palette similar to the one shown here or in a series of old saucers. Always mix more than you will need. If you have to stop to remix in the middle of a wash, it will be impossible to achieve a smooth satisfying effect. Ugly ridges will undoubtedly form. If you want a graded effect, mix two or three different strength solutions and work as shown in Plate 5, so that as you go down the piece of paper you can work from the strongest to the next strongest, and so on to achieve the lessening in your tone.

As you can see from the illustration, you should apply plenty of color. Keep a ridge of liquid moving down the paper as you work. Apply your brush with the lightest possible touch. It should hardly touch the paper at all, the drops of color forming underneath the brush as you guide the color down the piece of paper.

You are now ready to begin, and as water color is essentially a medium which is spontaneous—one that calls for quickness in application—a suitable subject can be a favorite landscape. Choose one that you know well, so that you will not have to think too deeply about it and can concentrate on your colors and brush strokes.

You will probably want to indicate the drawing lightly in pencil, or, for a more free and enjoyable approach, paint it in. Mix a very thin neutral gray from cobalt and burnt umber, and draw with this in a manner similar to that shown in Plate 6. The time of day for this picture was early afternoon when the sun was high in the sky. The time of year was October with a suggestion of bleakness in the atmosphere—not exactly a dismal day, but one slightly overcast. Concentrate on getting your basic lines. In this case the most important lines are the two converging edges of the bridge over the railroad yards. Next, pick up the vertical of the signal, and then start to work on the background of distant houses at the far end of the bridge.

See Plate 7. In the second stage quickly fix the truck in the foreground. Also vaguely indicate the figures. Their relation to other objects will give you a rough scale of size and thus help you establish the proper perspective. At this intermediary stage, don't attempt any fine detail. Keep your feeling broad; obtain the masses first, and strive to achieve the right tone values. Tone values or

Plate 6. Water color: first stage

Plate 7. Water color: second stage

Plate 8. Water color: completed

depths of color (regardless of hue) are the most important element of any picture.

In the second stage you can also begin the sky. Vaguely suggest it and bring along the blue areas and the patchy clouds, remembering to leave clear the space where the smoke from the steamy old locomotive will rise. In pure water color you should not use white or thick opaque colors. The whole picture should be in transparent colors and you should work from light to dark, the opposite of oils, where you tend to work from dark to light.

Having brought your picture to the second stage, proceed to the final touches, as in Plate 8. First of all you can further emphasize the wooden roadway by strengthening the tone in the foreground. Give some indication of the individual planks with broad strokes, perhaps picking up a few lines here and there from the moist color with the edge of a blotter. Keep the distant buildings and the roofs low in tone, verging toward blue-grays. You can give a slight emphasis to the windows in the high buildings at the end of the pier, but do not make them too strong. If you do, they will distract the eye from focusing properly on the composition.

The principal area of strength is almost central, with deep shadow underneath the platform canopies where the train is standing. If you make this shadow warm, almost purple in tint, it will strike a rich note against the yellow of the canopy itself, illustrating complementary harmony. You can strengthen the figures but do not give them too great an emphasis. Remember, they are only there to accentuate the recession and by their scale to assist the perspective of the picture. For a little accentuation on the signal and on the lampposts, a thin V-shaped highlight was cut out of the paper with a razor blade.

One temptation that you must resist is to take a water color too far. It is easy to go on fiddling with a small brush, picking up tiny details here, accentuating this or that. In a very short time you can spoil the freshness of your picture. It is much better to leave a water color (for that matter, a pastel, oil, or any form of picture) slightly unfinished. If you work at it too long, you may become tired unconsciously and will lose a sense of what you are doing. Try to train yourself to stop painting at just the right moment.

One great advantage the water-colorist has over the oil-painter is that to a certain extent he can choose his composition *after* he has painted his picture! Where the oil-painter has to paint to a fixed size, the water-colorist can manipulate when he has finished. In Plate 8 black lines indicate where the painting will be cropped. Not a great deal has been cut out, but the foreground has been shortened by about an inch, and a bit more taken off on the left.

There are a number of simple tricks which you can use successfully with water color. Plate 9 shows six examples.

No. 1: You can use a rubber or gum eraser on the paper to remove any amount of paint. You can use this technique for weakening a certain area, or, most effectively, for indicating rays of light from a lamp or sunbeams coming through a window into a dark room.

No. 2: Examples of razor-cut highlights similar to those in the painting we have just described in Plates 6-8. You must be a bit careful with this method if the paper is thin, but if you are using a thick paper, you will be surprised how strong an accent you can achieve.

No. 3: You can scrape sandpaper across the surface of the color to simulate such effects as rays of light, texture on a field, or rough stone. Of course, different grades of sandpaper will produce different effects.

No. 4: You can produce a speckled appearance by means of a wax resist. Rub a piece of ordinary paraffin or a wax candle lightly over the surface of rough paper. It will stick only to the raised portions of the paper and prevent them from absorbing color when you apply it. This process has many applications. You can use it on white paper or you can put one color on first, then wax and follow with a second color. This will produce a kind of two-toned appearance.

70

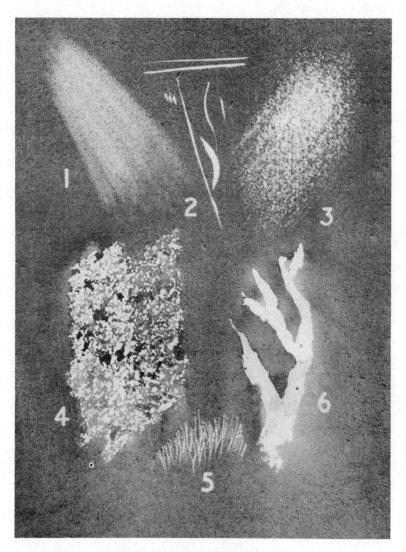

Plate 9. Water-color tricks

The effect shown in No. 5 is produced by scratching the surface of the paper with a needle, with the point of a compass, the point of a penknife blade, or some similar instrument. Use this technique for accentuating such things as rough, dry grass in a hayfield or light striking a railing.

No. 6 shows the use of latex to retain a white area when you are making a strong-toned wash. Sometimes it is difficult to guide the wash around an intricate shape such as the old tree trunk roughly indicated here. Apply latex with a knife blade or brush and allow to set for 5 or 10 minutes. Now you can wash the color right over not only the paper but also the latex itself. After the wash is dry remove the latex with a gum or rubber eraser, exposing the pure white paper underneath. You can use this device with dramatic effect in night scenes where you want some very bright highlights in the foreground, as you might in painting a fair or a circus. Use it, too, for glazing streaks on a window, or for an immediate contrast of dark and light tones which would be difficult to obtain by normal methods.

Water color is essentially a strong, bright method of painting which succeeds best if it is done directly and kept broad in treatment. Correction is nearly impossible to achieve, but if you want to attempt it, use a brush with lots of clean water and softly scrub the area to be changed with a circular motion. You might also try a gentle application of sandpaper. Unless the mistake is a glaring one, however, it is generally best to leave it.

Always remember that to achieve the sparkle and purity which make water colors so delightful it is essential to keep your brush as clean as possible all the time. Always have lots of clean water on hand. If you go out-of-doors to paint from nature be sure to take plenty of water with you.

VI

OPAQUE AND TEXTURE PAINTING

It's fun to work and experiment with what is called gouache. This simply means working in a water-based medium, as opposed to oils or tempera, and using opaque as well as transparent colors. You can also introduce the impasto and thick brush effects possible with oil. Such methods of painting offer the greatest scope for experiment and, within reason, anything goes.

The materials you need will not necessarily run you into further large expense. To start with, you can use ordinary water colors with one of the thick opaque whites which are available. At the dealer's you can find a wide variety of these whites for use with water color. Included are some that are specially prepared to produce impasto effects that will stand up in the same manner as oil paints. There are also cakes of opaque colors to go with these whites, and they are very inexpensive. With them you can achieve approximate water color effects as well as those of the heavier gouache and texture painting. All you need do is to mix the heavy white with your other colors and apply them in a manner that resembles oil painting (described in Chapter VII) more than the method used for water coloring.

You can use either hair or bristle brushes. Those which you have already bought for water color or oil will be quite serviceable, and the various characteristics of the different shapes and types can be brought into use.

If you wish further to supplement the colors you already have, you can buy tubes of poster color which will help you achieve richer and stronger textures. Tubes are probably preferable to pots of poster color, for they tend to keep the color moist longer. Also, there is no danger of mixing one color with another through accidentally dipping a brush which is already being used into a clean jar of color.

The papers you can use are the same as for water color. You can bring into service a very wide range indeed, from inexpensive coarse ones to art cover papers. These are the range of hard-surfaced, extremely serviceable papers in bright colors, admirable backgrounds upon which to build up exciting pictures. For example, if you start a fairground scene on a sheet of deep crimson, it is surprising how a few strokes of bright lights can suggest the general scene.

Painting on brightly colored papers can be very exciting and open up whole new treatments for you. The art cover paper mentioned is quite reasonable in price, and comes in sheets 22 by 30, which when halved or quartered will provide an excellent ground for you to work on. Papers come in many weights, qualities and sizes, all of which result in interesting finished paintings.

Your palette for gouache must be roomy. You can use a muffin tin similar to the palette illustrated in Plate 5, a sheet of glass, saucers, old plates or anything which will hold a large amount of color. The essence of this type of painting is plenty of paint. Don't be stingy! Mix with a certain amount of care, and as directly as possible but don't "over-puddle" the colors or they will lose their bright, vigorous tints and become drab.

Start a painting of this type with a bit of preliminary brush or pencil drawing to get the approximate massing of your subject. After the preliminaries are completed, keep the treatment free and as full of expression as you wish to make it. Plate 10 shows a heavily textured painting of a prickly cactus plant. This is how it was done: First, the background tint was mixed and brushed on

Plate 10. Texture painting

very thickly. As it began to set, a coarse comb was dragged through it vertically to produce the ridges you see. The same treatment was used for the surface on which the pot is resting, except that the comb was dragged horizontally. When this background color was skin-dry, that is, when the surface of the paint became hard, the pot itself was drawn with a hog hair brush, and then layered over with a small palette knife used to scrape one color across another in a bold manner. Next, the cactus was put in as a dark green shape and left to dry. Then, with a No. 1 hog and black paint it was outlined on the right side, away from the light. Later, again with a small knife, light green was placed on the left side and the main body of the cactus brought out by this use of light and shade. When this was dry, a small palette knife loaded first with white and later with black was used on its edge to put the prickles on the cactus. Finally when the whole was quite hard and dry, the light was scraped across on the left and the deep shadows placed into position on the right.

This is just one example of texture treatment for painting in this manner. It should show you some of the possibilities for experimentation. All manner of things can be used for effect, not only combs but also such objects as old nail brushes, sponges, cut corks and rough rags. Each technique will produce a new, exciting result. You can put on the paint itself with hard or soft bristle brushes or scrape it on with a knife, rub it on with your finger, or spatter it by loading an old nail brush with color, rubbing your finger through it so that tiny drops of color fly off onto the paper.

You will enjoy experimenting for varied effects. Work on rough pieces of paper or cards, practicing patterns with combs, small knives and other implements. See how great a variety of strokes you can produce with your brushes, particularly the hog. Try holding the brush underhand or crosswise to change the direction of the bristles.

In opaque and texture painting you can let yourself go with unusual color contrasts, vigorously used. The complementary system will produce brilliant results. For example, the background of the prickly cactus is bright red and reacts well against the light greens of the plant.

The slight strengthening of a normal water color by mixing opaque white with other colors to achieve darker and richer tones is also a challenge. At first you can attempt slight accents of strength here and there. Later use these intense colors on buildings, or trees; you will be surprised at how vividly they stand out against the more limpid tones of the background.

If you want to be really explosive, try using poster colors or the cheaper powder colors mixed with plaster of Paris. This will give you a very thick paint for building up a thick impasto. Use either hardboard or paper stuck onto a piece of hardboard or three-ply wood, so the paper will be able to carry the weight of the paint. Don't expect permanence, for a picture treated in this wild manner will last only a few months before cracking. This method is fun, and you can probably learn a good deal about texture and color, but it is not to be considered for serious work.

For another interesting and instructive project dabble with mixed techniques—a combination of two or more of the regular media. For example, oil over a tempera underpainting will last quite well. You can even let part of the tempera show through with perfect safety. Try tempera on top of oils for further interesting results.

Mixing media in the water-color technique opens up extremely interesting and exciting fields. Each medium has its own possibilities and, by using two or more combined, the liveliest features of each can often be incorporated. Start your picture as a pure water color and then bring in not only gouache but also accents of pastel, charcoal or India ink. The finished result will have an individual character all its own, but you must work with a light touch. Don't put on too heavy a pastel, for instance, or too thick an impasto.

When your pictures are finished there are several methods you can apply as a final treatment. Paper varnish will bring up the colors, greatly enhancing the lights and further enriching the dark tones. It will also change the nature of the paper itself when it is covered with thin colors, the varnish tending to make it semi-transparent. Therefore, before applying the varnish, try it out over some color on scraps of paper to make sure it doesn't alter the tone values enough to throw your picture out of balance.

Another finishing method is to apply wax as a polish. You can buy it in jars from your dealer. It has an advantage over varnish in that, while it brings up the colors, it makes very little tonal difference to your picture. Rub the wax on sparingly, or if your painting is particularly thick and full of ridges, apply it with a soft brush to make sure that it gets into all the crevices. Let it dry for about half an hour, and then rub it smartly to bring up the polish.

One word of warning about very heavily painted pictures: Although they dry quite speedily, they are easily affected by excessive humidity in the atmosphere. Therefore, it is unwise to put them in a portfolio, for on a rainy day they will become sticky, and not only will they be ruined themselves, they are also likely to damage the drawings next to them.

VII

PAINTING IN OILS

After you have explored some of the possibilities of water color and texture painting, you will undoubtedly wish to try oils. No other way of painting can give quite the richness and the range in color, tone and effect that oils produce. Perhaps that is why the majority of great pictures of past and present have been painted in this medium. You may even wish to start with oil painting before trying other methods.

Oil painting is not as old a method as water coloring; it was not perfected until the fifteenth century, when two Flemish painters, Hugo and Jan Van Eyck, carried out their exploratory work. Since their time many artists have experimented further and increased the range of this rich medium.

Oil paint lends itself to a great variety of uses. For example, you can paint it on thinly, almost like water color, diluting the pigments with turpentine. You can paint in the standard method, using bristle brushes to spread fairly thick layers of paint, or using both hair and bristle brushes for a combination of effects. You can create pictures using only little trowellike palette knives. Or, if you wish, you can underpaint first in tempera (see page 55). This method was in vogue with many of the early artists as it produces great stability. Again, you can paint your composition as a monochrome in opaque pigments, and then dilute transparent colors with oils which will have a waterlike transparency. Like many contemporary artists, you can also use thick ridges of paint to achieve various textures. These are called impasto. With oil paint you can use almost any type of brushwork you wish.

When you purchase your oil paints, you can either buy a ready-filled box or choose your own colors. As with other methods of painting, it is the best policy to start with as few colors as possible. Many of the finest artists of the past worked with a very limited palette. If you buy two or three dozen different colors, the chances are that you will buy some which will not work satisfactorily together or, even worse, may be harmful to each other, causing darkening, cracking or some other form of discoloration. Second, you will have far more colors than you can quickly master.

Understanding and knowing your paints is of prime importance with oil painting. Each color has certain definite characteristics when used by itself, but these may change when intermixed with others. Some colors when mixed or "broken" with white will change their basic tone and tint; white mixed with black will often give surprising results.

The following pigments will serve you well for a long time and are quite capable of producing all the different effects which you may desire: cadmium yellow, yellow ochre, cadmium red, Indian red, alizarin crimson, ultramarine, oxide of chromium and raw umber. Besides these you will need a large tube of white, preferably titanium. This is a satisfactory, powerful, clean, white which is non-poisonous, covers well and is a good mixer.

If you are buying loose tubes, it is economical to buy them as large as possible, because they are cheaper that way. Also, it will tend to encourage you to paint thickly and get the most from this exciting medium.

The different types of brushes have been discussed in Chapter IV. If you wish, you can get a ready-selected set. Otherwise, a good choice is: short flat bristle brushes (Nos. 4, 6, and 8) and at least two flat sable brushes, preferably No. 10 and No. 12. You can profitably add what is termed a "rigger."

You can either buy a palette or use a piece of plywood or masonite. (Give the plywood a thorough soaking in linseed oil before you use it, or else the dry wood will suck out most of the binding oils.) If you are painting indoors, a sheet of glass on a table with white paper underneath makes an excellent palette that is easy to clean at the end of the painting session. You can even buy a palette of disposable sheets of oil-resistant paper.

Before you start any serious painting, spend some time experimenting with your various brushes and also with all your different colors. Plate 11 shows a few examples of brush strokes in oil made with a bristle. No. 1 was done with a small, round brush, and the color was diluted with copal oil medium or linseed oil. You can use this brush for long, curving strokes or for crisp short strokes.

No. 2 shows how a bristle brush was used to simulate leaf forms. This type of brush with its carefully modeled head will provide you with great control over the paint.

No. 3 shows how a large, flat brush might be used for a sky. In oils, if you have a large area to cover, avoid at all costs, the long up-and-down or horizontal strokes that a house painter would use. You don't want ugly ridges of paint which will catch unnecessary reflections. Little, short, crosshatched strokes will provide the flat cover needed.

No. 4 shows how you can use a large, round brush to produce small, round shapes. These might be water-lily leaves or centers of flowers, and they are made by holding the brush almost at right angles to the canvas and twirling it between the finger and thumb.

No. 5 was also done with a large, round brush. Here it was used almost dry with very little color on it, and stippled up and down.

No. 6 shows how you can use a flat brush to do the drawing and painting in one step. Here, short, vertical strokes with a well-loaded brush produce brick or stone formation.

In No. 7, the color has been rubbed in with the finger to produce an absolutely flat surface.

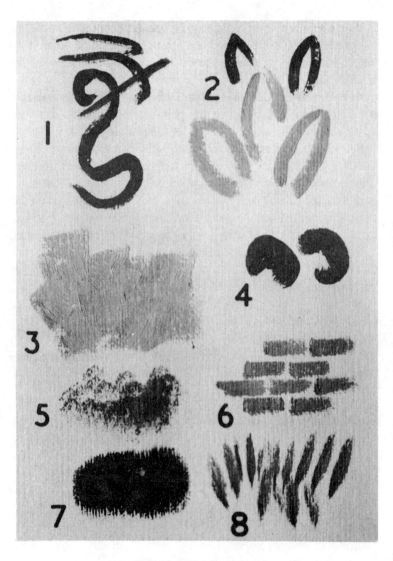

Plate 11. Oil brush strokes

No. 8, again, shows the flat brush used in short, sharp, vertical strokes to portray what might be heavy grass in the foreground of a picture or some other form of plant life.

Experiment with your brushes and colors until you grow familiar with them. Try out different mixes to see what they will produce, so that, when you begin to paint, you will quickly be able to get the particular tones and tints you are seeking. You will make many fascinating discoveries. For instance, alizarin crimson, ultramarine and raw umber together will give you great depths of color.

Ultramarine and raw umber will produce a very deep green.

Cadmium yellow mixed with cadmium red will produce a brilliant, strong orange.

Indian red and yellow ochre will produce a dull orange, suitable in some cases for brickwork.

Try a very small amount of Prussian blue or ultramarine mixed with white for skies. A sky is not always pure blue, however, and certainly not at the horizon. So as you come down, bring into your blue more white, a little yellow ochre and just a touch of crimson. Pinkishness is characteristic of the horizon due to the refraction of light from clouds of fine dust which are present in the air.

Try different varieties of green by mixing cadmium yellow and ultramarine; yellow ochre and ultramarine; cadmium yellow and oxide of chromium, or yellow ochre and oxide of chromium.

Raw umber with different amounts of white will produce a beautiful range of light browns and near-grays, extremely useful in the background of flower painting and also in stonework on old buildings. You can also make a true gray from yellow ochre, Indian red and ultramarine with varying amounts of white for the depth of tone needed. Alizarin crimson will yield a great variety of pinks when you mix it in different proportions with titanium white. Purple will come from crimson and ultramarine. You will be able to make an almost endless list of variations and tints by experimenting with your colors in different combinations and different proportions.

For your first work, oil-painting papers will be quite satisfactory. They will enable you to get most of the effects which are possible on a canvas board or stretched canvas. Since pads of these papers are inexpensive, you can use them freely. Later, you will graduate to canvas on board and eventually to stretch canvas on a wooden frame.

Besides colors, brushes, palette and ground, you will need a small bottle of either linseed oil or copal oil medium for diluting colors; a bottle of turpentine for washing the brushes and palette at the end of the day; a bundle of rags and lastly, an easel. True, you can arrange a makeshift easel indoors by putting a box against which to lean your canvas board on the table, or out-of-doors, by propping your board against the trunk of a fallen tree, a branch, a wall or a gate. But as soon as you can, get some form of easel for yourself. For then you can go to work wherever you want. An easel can be adjusted and will hold your canvas steady.

For oil painting, it is wisest to start with an indoor subject. As we have seen, landscape painting poses the problem of changing light and its effect on color. At first oil painting itself will be strange and will appear difficult. Since oils are not particularly fluid, managing them will take a great deal of concentration. For a while you will have to give more effort to manipulating the paint than to capturing your subject dramatically.

To begin, arrange a still life. Don't think, however, that a still life need be a dull collection of objects. In Plate 15 some puppets representing characters from *Alice in Wonderland*, old dolls and toys, make an interesting composition. In your first effort, aim for something simple. Don't give yourself too many problems of light and shade. Remember the hints on general composition in the earlier chapters. Watch that principal shapes are not cut up by the edge of the picture or placed too near an edge; see that the composition is neither unbalanced nor too symmetrically arranged; and make sure it gives a feeling of harmony. At first glance you may think the figures in Plate 15 have been grouped without a great deal of forethought, but a moment's study will reveal that they all fit very comfortably into what might be termed an adequate composition. There is nothing striking about the arrangement, yet it gives a pleasant feeling.

When you have set up your group, you are ready to begin painting. Your paper, prepared board, or canvas board is in place on the easel, or leaning against a box on the table. Now, load your palette with the colors, carefully squeezing them from the bottom of the tube. Place them near the edge, as in Fig. 32, and always in the same order, for you will save a great deal of time later on if you know exactly where to find each color. Put out more white than other colors. Pour some turpentine (painters usually shorten this to "turps") into the tin cup which is attached to your easel, or into a handy jar.

In mixing oils, try not to clog your brushes. If you find the color on your palette becoming muddy, scrape it off with a palette knife,

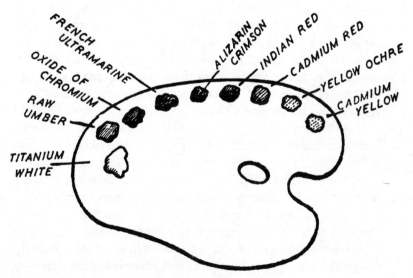

Fig. 32. Arrangement of colors on the palette

and squeeze out fresh color in a clean place. If your colors are muddy, they will lose their brightness, sparkle and vigor. Clean your brushes thoroughly between colors, rinsing them two or three times in turps and pulling them through your rag. If your palette becomes dirty, clean it thoroughly. Often fresh, clean colors will give you renewed inspiration!

Take your palette in your hand, or stand close to your sheet of glass on the table. In your left hand hold your spare brushes and your rag. Stand back from your model; look at it carefully and for quite a long time until you feel the basic shapes of the composition which you have arranged imprinted on your mind. With your brush well moistened with turpentine, mix up a thin, diluted neutral gray, almost of water-color consistency. Use titanium white, ultramarine and raw umber.

Now you are ready to paint.

Plate 12, the first stage of the still life, demonstrates the first brush strokes you use in putting a composition on canvas. Notice how broad and simple they are. At this stage any attempt to capture minute details would only worry you and might cause the picture to lose balance. Instead, go right ahead and draw the principal shapes in boldly: the jug, the figures, the bottle, the crisscross of the string holder and the teapot. Keep it as simple as this first illustration. In the second picture the drawing, as such, has been completed.

Many artists and teachers advocate the preparation of a very careful pencil or charcoal underdrawing, correct in every detail, before applying any oil. This may have advantages, but it also has disadvantages. For instance, if you draw with charcoal, you will have to "fix" it before you paint; otherwise, it will mix with the colors. Second, careful drawing does tend to constrict the painting that will follow. To be successful, oil painting must be direct. The direct approach goes well back into history. Titian, Rubens, Constable, the Impressionists, and still later men of the stature of Augustus John go right in with the brush, and fulfill with strong,

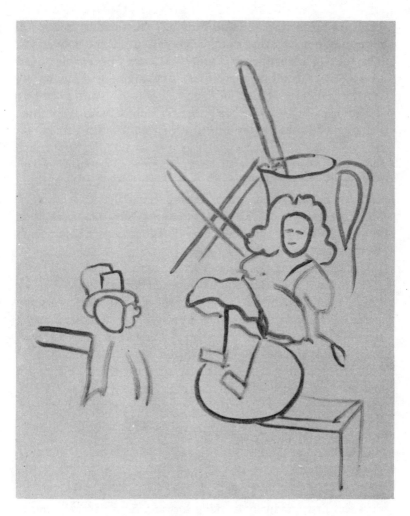

Plate 12. Oil painting: first stage

rich strokes the purpose of oil painting. The timid approach will never produce satisfying results. Oils cry out for the bold attack. The gusto of artists such as Turner and Frans Hals enabled them to exploit to the full the powerful expression of this medium.

After you have sketched in the brush drawing, swiftly brush in the principal areas with color slightly diluted with turpentine. Painting with color that is diluted with a spirit rather than with a heavy oil, such as linseed, copal or poppy, is said to be "lean," and the rule is to paint "fat over lean." The reason is that if you put two layers of thick oil color one upon the other, they are likely to dry at different speeds, thus causing eventual severe cracking. So dilute your underpainting with turpentine and brush it in quickly. It will dry in a short period of time, and you can begin overpainting.

Underpainting in this manner serves, too, to point up any error of judgment in the placement of shapes and objects at the drawing stage. Often when the picture is partially colored, such errors will stand out. If a correction is needed now—or at the earlier drawing stage—it is very simple to moisten a corner of your rag with turpentine and to rub out the undesired parts.

If you want to achieve a thick texture, use the oil paint, stiff and short, as it comes from the tube. But as you can see from Plate 11, brushwork is largely a matter of personal discovery. From your own experiments and from your experience, you will develop an individual style.

Now, look at Plate 13.

First work at your background. Whatever the method of painting you are using, it is always the wisest course to paint the distances first, gradually working forward. This will help you to achieve an illusion of recession. So, first put in the background and the table on which the objects are standing, the dark of the inside of the drawer and the darkness underneath the drawer. After you have brushed in these areas, you can begin with the bottle, jug and teapot. Paint them in their true colors, but always

Plate 13. Oil painting: second stage

Plate 14. Oil painting: third stage

watch for tone. As we pointed out on page 29, tone is in many ways more important than color. To get the relationships correct, look at your painting with half-closed eyes.

In Plate 14 the picture is nearly finished. Highlights, patches of shadow and details such as the eyes on the puppets are left out for the moment. Concentrate on getting the whole picture into balance; then make any necessary corrections of drawing. After this stage a correction, although still possible, will be difficult and is likely to destroy the freshness of the finished result.

At last, in Plate 15 we come to the final details: the spots on Alice's frock, the eyes, the bells, etc. Add a few soft reflections in the bottle at the back, an indication of shadows on the drapes and make some attempt at graining, to give a feeling of substance to the wood itself.

Finally at this stage when your tones presumably are correct, you can concentrate on trying to achieve the different textures of the various objects you are painting: try to catch the hard gloss of the teapot, the glitter of the bottle, the soft wooly tow color of Alice's hair, the crumbly texture of the cake. Even now, don't be tempted to use a sable brush to put in too many finicky details. By all means use it for the eyebrows, the eyes and perhaps one or two stripes on the March Hare's trousers, but resist the temptation to go on daubing away at the canvas. Too much unimportant detail will kill the freshness and spontaneity of your subject.

You should be able to complete a still life in a couple of sittings. On the first day try to finish the underpainting and the rough drawing. Then on the second day your picture will be dry, and you can apply your thick paint, work at getting your tone values correct and put in the texture, highlights and the final little flicks of color which will bring a picture to life.

Don't just attack the picture haphazardly, painting every portion with equal strength, equal amounts of detail and highlights or it will lose power. Emphasize only what is most interesting: the blacks of Alice's shoes, the teapot spout outlined against the cross

Plate 15. Oil painting: completed

of the string holder, the lights on the hare's ears. But in addition, if you highlighted the knife handle heavily, increased the highlights on the bottle and the depth of tone behind the teapot, probably you upset the balance of the picture. At all stages of your painting, bear in mind the simple rules of composition and control mentioned in Chapter II.

Leave your completed picture to dry leaning against a wall face inward so that dust won't fall on the sticky paint. When it is "skin-dry," the surface of the paint dry to the touch, it is safe to frame it and hang it. At this stage don't attempt to varnish the surface even though it appears dry to the touch, for the oil in the thickest areas will not have hardened completely. An oil painting should not be varnished for at least nine months; it is better to leave it for a whole year. At that time, dust it and wipe it with a swab of absorbent cotton dipped in turpentine. Varnish it on a warm, dry day either with a mastic, damar, or better still one of the new clear synthetic varnishes.

If for some reason such as an exhibition or some other special event, you wish to brighten up your picture before it has been varnished, you can lightly brush it with "retouching varnish." This is a weak solution of resin which will brighten up the colors, but will not put an impervious seal over them which would prevent the oils from drying out properly. Retouching varnish or medium is also useful if you begin a picture and have to leave it for a few days; when you come back to the painting, brush this varnish over the areas which have dried out in an unpleasantly flat manner.

When you visit your art dealer's you may see some small trowel-like knives. These are painting knives. After you have begun to master the manipulation of paint with a brush, buy one or two of these knives and attempt painting with them. It can be quite a useful exercise in directness. To start with, the most suitable subject would be a still life, perhaps a simple bowl of roses or chrysanthemums. It is a good plan to light the model powerfully from one side, so that there will be strong contrasts of light and shade.

For knife painting load your palette generously. This method does require a considerable amount of paint. The secret is to mix colors as little as possible and to apply them with a direct touch.

Do your initial drawing-in the same way as for an ordinary brush painting but before you begin you will find it helpful to stain your white canvas board or white paper with a coat of raw umber and Indian red, diluted with turpentine. Allow it to dry overnight. In knife painting it is difficult to cover every portion of the canvas, and it is disturbing if too many pieces of sparkling white show through between strokes. The various colors sit much more harmoniously on the tinted ground. Many painters have used this method.

When your drawing-in is completed, take up your painting knife and mix your colors on the palette. Apply them with direct and sweeping strokes, working the background first. Plate 16 shows some of the different effects you can produce with the painting knife. In No. 1 the knife has been loaded along the edges to produce sharp, straight lines.

To get the effect pictured in No. 2, take up a good deal of paint on the underside of the knife and place it down sharply on the canvas to produce little leaflike strokes. You might use these for roses or other plants.

For No. 3, smear a thick layer of paint onto the ground, and bring the knife down with short, sharp, lifting strokes. You will produce a series of thick ridges useful for depicting tiles, rough stonework or some similar texture.

For No. 4, load the knife with small amounts of several different colors, and swing it around in a straightforward smearing stroke. This is useful for painting water, or for areas which need a variegated but smooth surface.

Place a fair amount of paint on the ground for No. 5. Then drag

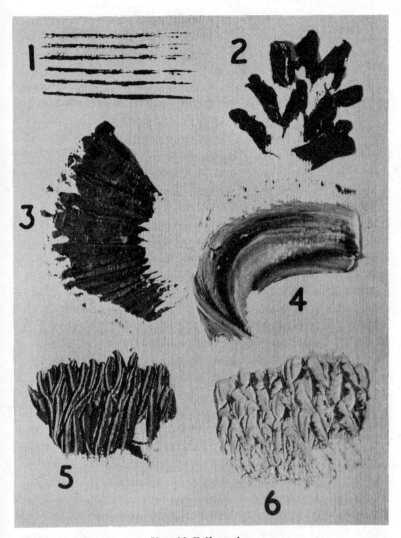

Plate 16. Knife strokes

the point of the knife through it. This method could be employed to achieve the texture of grass, for example, or forms of foliage.

Lastly, in No. 6, the paint has once more been applied to the ground first. You then stipple it by placing the knife down into the color and lifting it straight up from the canvas. You can use this dappled effect for grass, a field, or rough textures in buildings.

Remember these techniques as you approach your flower piece, and use some of the illustrated methods. The broad smearing stroke might be good for the background and perhaps for the table on which the vase stands. Try other strokes for the foliage of the plants. For example, for a chrysanthemum smear on the color in the general shape of the bloom, then indicate the petals by dragging the point of the knife through the paint.

Knife painting—attractive, fresh and vigorous as it is—can be difficult. Don't be discouraged if your first effort results in a large expanse of mud. Don't be tempted to mix your color on the canvas, for you should always do it on the palette. To achieve sparkle and purity of color does require practice and care, not only in the mixing but also in placing the paint precisely on the canvas. Now, leave it alone!

Studying the works of great artists is both pleasant and rewarding, and you can learn a lot even from black-and-white reproductions. In this book landscapes by four different artists illustrate greatly differing approaches. We have already learned a lot about composition from studying "The Avenue, Middelharnis" (Plate 1) by Hobbema (page 32).

John Constable's famous "Hay Wain" (Plate 17) is one of the loveliest of all renderings of the English countryside. Constable very seldom chose complicated scenes for his compositions. He was often content with the simple countryside near his home. Here, a little farmhouse or mill stands beside a quietly flowing river. The horizontal line of the river is gently broken for the viewer by the careful placing of the hay wain itself, as the horses stand in the stream cooling themselves after the day's work. Constable was a master at achieving the realism of nature. In his treatment of foliage, what appears from the distance to be

Plate 17. "The Hay Wain" by John Constable (1776-1836)

meticulous treatment, dissolves on close approach into great
breadth and power of surely placed brush strokes.

The field on the other side of the river illustrates another
masterful touch. Notice how it recedes with great ease and flatness
toward the distant woods. Achieving flatness in a plane going off
into the distance sometimes presents a problem. The use of warm
color in the foreground and a recession toward cool blue tones
in the background is one good solution. Compare the sky in this
picture with that of Hobbema in Plate 1. You can see how much
the English landscape painter owed to the earlier work of this
Dutchman. His beautiful masses of white clouds are echoed in
this later work of Constable's.

Pissarro was one of the French Impressionists who, as their
name implies, sought to catch an impression rather than photo-

Plate 18. "Le Louvre, Matin, Neige" by Camille Pissarro (1830-1903)

graphic exactness. See Plate 18, "Le Louvre, Matin, Neige." For all its lack of detail and its roughness of treatment in the immediate foreground of the courtyard, it gives a wonderful feeling of a cold, snowy day in Paris. The tone values of the snow itself on the distant buildings, on the bridge, the wall and in the foreground are exactly right. Pissarro realized that in the dusty, often murky, yellow atmosphere of a winter's day in a great city, the snow would not gleam white but would take on a yellow tinge.

It is interesting to compare his treatment of trees with Constable's use of strong shadow and with Hobbema's delicate tracery. Pissarro's trees appear just as strong as do those of the other two artists. Although his treatment may at first appear vague, his values and tones are so correct that they result in an extremely convincing illusion of reality.

Another famous landscape is one by an American who worked most of his life in London, James McNeill Whistler. Whistler was an artist of great refinement and a man who worked with a very limited palette. His two famous portraits, one of his mother and one of the writer Thomas Carlyle, are so delicate that they are almost monochromes of gray. With his consummate skill Whistler could produce great variety of effect from limited resources.

Whistler's "Battersea Bridge" (Plate 19) was the subject of much controversy in the last century. In it he rejected the usual compositional shapes for a landscape and used a most unlikely form—a capital T. Yet he brings the strong mass of the tall upright of the bridge and its cross-span under control by the delicate tone values of the bridge against the sky. The section of bridge frames the main interests of the picture, the beautifully painted lights reflected on the water and the fireworks shooting through the pale limpid sky. The foreground is bare except for a solitary figure on a raft or pontoon.

Plate 19. "Battersea Bridge" by James McNeill Whistler (1834-1903)

Even a slight change in composition would destroy the delicate balance of "Battersea Bridge." Fig. 33 shows what might have happened if the principal pillar had been carried a little further to the left. At once there is a feeling of tension, as if something might

Fig. 33. Altered composition of Whistler's painting destroys the harmony, balance and beauty

fall from the span of the bridge. This is further emphasized by the incorrect placing of the figures. The one on the raft or boat now coincides with the reflection of the upright and is almost completely lost. The fireworks are so spread out that they are no longer dramatic.

Whistler painted this picture almost entirely in soft greens, grays and blues. The only touches of brightness are the bursting rockets, the reflected lights on the right and one or two windows in the buildings on the left. Yet, for all this simplicity of treatment Whistler has achieved a beautiful harmony with this canvas.

Constable, Hobbema, Pissarro and Whistler, working in different countries at different times, produced four strikingly different approaches to landscape. Yet in some ways the four are similar.

Each man is obviously sincere, and each has seen his picture through a highly individual eye.

After you have painted two or three still lifes or flower pieces indoors, you can proceed with landscape. Use the technical hints you have learned for brush work and mixing colors. Before you start to paint, however, concentrate on the scene until you can see it with your eyes closed. And when you begin, keep to broad masses as long as you can. Only when you have perfected these, should you proceed to the finer details.

VIII

PASTELS, CHARCOAL, PENCIL, INK AND SCRATCHBOARD

PASTELS

Often erroneously called crayons or chalks, pastels are actually sticks composed of pure pigments mixed with varying quantities of an inert white material such as kaolin. The binding matter varies, but it is always kept to the minimum. For example, the casein in skim milk will produce a form of weak glue to bind together the elements of a pastel stick.

The use of pastels is comparatively modern; it was not until the seventeenth century that professional artists began to use them. The pastel, if used directly and with care, produces a very pleasant, bright, clean effect because the pigment is so nearly pure.

If you decide to try this somewhat difficult method of painting, you will need a fairly large box of pastels. Because pastels are most effective when put on directly (that is, with no mixing), your box should contain at least three dozen shades. You should get a pastel box with softly padded partitions to prevent the sticks from rolling against each other. You will also need a few paper stumps (for spreading or blending color), and a bristle brush will be useful.

The papers for pastel are various, and include a range of fine rag papers sometimes called Ingres. Tinted papers come in a wide selection of pleasant shades for undercolors. Many other makes are also on the market, among which are the fine-grained sandpapers and varying degrees of gray, brown, fawn and blue thin but rough-textured papers.

Your underdrawing should consist of only a few bare, pale pencil lines. Do it in pastels. Use the strokes of the pastel in a manner similar to the strokes of your brush in oil painting. Scumble the sky and background on with your finger by putting a few strokes of the pastel on the paper and then rubbing the color lightly to form a smooth ground. Or, if you prefer, rub with a paper stump, or brush in with the bristle brush. As you work toward the foreground use stronger, more definite strokes. Leave them untouched to build up your various textures.

Correction is extremely difficult, but if you must, use either an art eraser or a kneaded eraser. The latter is probably better because you can knead and point it into any particular shape you want. It will also serve to pick out a highlight or to bring up a line that needs to be lightened.

In pastel as in water color, it is best to work from light to dark. Do not complete any single section individually; rather, work on the whole composition, watching the tone values carefully. Try to put your strokes in the right place the first time, for that is how to achieve the ultimate sparkle of this attractive medium. Pastel is particularly suitable for landscapes. The brightness of the medium and the speed at which you can work enable you to capture even the fleeting lights of a bright sunny day.

If you are working on a building, as in Plate 20, treat your stonework as you would if you were working with oils; use the stick of pastel as a brush, firmly drawing one tone beside another. As you work, be very careful not to touch the drawing with your hand or sleeve, especially after you have put your last touches into place. It is all too easy to brush against the surface of the picture; in a few seconds you can ruin an afternoon's careful work!

After your picture is finished, it is extremely fragile; not only will it smudge if a hand is brushed over it, but even a jolt may loosen part of the pastel powder. Until recently many artists

Plate 20. Using pastels

refused to use fixative on their drawings, preferring to have them carefully framed. They felt that the use of a fixative would disturb the colors. You may have seen pastel drawings hanging with a layer of powdered color along the bottom of the mount. Such drawings were not fixed.

Today's fixatives are colorless, having only a negligible effect on tone and tint. It is best, therefore, to fix your picture thoroughly when you have finished it. You can use a mouth spray like the one next to the bottle in Plate 20. Open it to a right-angle shape, put the long leg into the bottle of fixative and blow through the little mouthpiece. This produces a fine spray of fixative, which you should direct carefully over the drawing from a distance of about

12 to 18 inches. Never overload the drawing or soak it; you will lose the whole crisp effect of a pastel. If the drawing becomes too wet, it will take on the appearance of a gouache or opaque painting. Since the tiny particles of color will flow together, the colors themselves will lose the values which you originally gave them. Instead, put on two or three light applications, allowing plenty of drying time between each.

CHARCOAL

Charcoal, one of the cheapest media available, can give you extraordinary satisfaction. A simple stick of charcoal is capable of producing immense subtleties and ranges of tone and effect. The most suitable paper is a fairly thin-grained rag similar to that used for pastels, although rougher-textured tinted papers will also take the medium satisfactorily.

Use your charcoal immediately, even for the undersketch as you did with pastels. But use it lightly. Hold it loosely and draw with great tenderness. Charcoal, like pastel, is difficult to correct, especially if it is in a dark, strong tone. So again work from light to dark. You can use a paper stump or your finger for blending. The bristle brush will also serve, and the gum eraser or kneaded eraser will take out highlights. (See Plate 21.)

When the drawing is completed, fix it in the same manner as a pastel. Use even more care not to soak the surface with the spray, because the charcoal particles will very easily flow together, spoiling the drawing with ugly streaks.

PENCIL

Undoubtedly the most useful implement you possess is the humble pencil. It is used at all stages of your work, in your sketch book, for underdrawing and for giving accents in opaque painting.

If you are doing a pencil drawing by itself as a finished work, the most important thing to remember is to keep the point sharp. A drawing done with a blunt point lacks crispness, sensitivity and

Plate 21. Use of stump with charcoal

feeling. It is difficult to sharpen a very soft pencil without breaking the point. The best way to do it is to pare the wood with a knife and sharpen the point with sandpaper, so keep both handy.

Hold the pencil lightly; don't grip it fiercely. Pencil drawing, like any form of painting, is an act of great sensitivity. Therefore, do not hold that pencil or brush too tightly, for if you do, the drawing will appear harsh and labored.

You can produce light and shade in a pencil drawing in several ways. The softer grades will lend themselves to stumping or scumbling in the manner of charcoal. Medium grades such as 2B can be used with varieties of crosshatching to achieve the different depths of tone you are seeking. An even more subtle approach is to vary your thickness of line. You can show the direction of light on a plant, for example, by indicating the side nearest the sun by the merest thread of delicately drawn pencil. For the shaded side, use a softer pencil and slightly increased pressure.

Soft pencil drawings should be fixed to prevent smudging. Drawings made with harder grades do not have to be fixed, but a light spray can do no harm.

INK

In one form or another, people have been drawing with inks for a very long time, even before the monks used them for illuminating manuscripts. Today you can either buy waterproof or water-soluble ink. When you are buying ink, make sure you obtain the type you need. The waterproof variety is intended for use in conjunction with water color, to be finished with a wash.

Pen drawing gives scope for considerable experimentation, because an amazing assortment of different nibs is available. These range from the tiniest steel nibs up to one-inch-wide poster pens. Some shops still offer sharpened turkey and chicken feather quills, and occasionally one can come across a reed pen, although these are extremely rare.

It is best to execute a pen-and-ink drawing over a fairly careful pencil sketch. Whether you draw with waterproof ink or soluble, it is nearly impossible to make satisfactory corrections. If you make a mistake, you can try scraping it out with a razor blade or some other sharp instrument, or with sandpaper, but you must exercise great care to avoid damaging the paper.

Indicate light and shade either by crosshatching, varying the thickness of your lines or by a combination of crosshatching and the use of a soft hair brush. A pen-and-ink drawing combined with a brush wash can possess great power and richness (see Fig. 34). (If you use a brush with ink, be very careful to wash it out thoroughly afterwards, because ink can rot the hairs in a very short space of time.)

Fig. 34. Pen, brush and ink

SCRATCHBOARD

A comparatively new material, scratchboard is widely used in commercial art, book illustrations and advertising in general—whenever clean, crisp, strong black-and-white drawings are needed. It consists of cardboard covered with a thin layer of plaster or chalk. Most scratchboard has a layer of black sprayed over it, but a white variety is also available.

As the name implies, you work on the board by scratching the material, exposing the brilliant white of the plaster layer underneath the dull black finish. Fig. 35 shows some of the strokes and effects you can obtain with scratchboard knives. These small,

Fig. 35. Strokes and textures with scratchboard

niblike knives come in a variety of shapes, and each knife produces different effects according to how you hold it. You must be careful, however, not to penetrate beyond the plaster into the cardboard.

With white scratchboard you first work up a pen-and-ink or brush drawing. When the ink dries, you can use a knife on the black portions to produce a combination of engraved and drawn effects. Fig. 36 is an example of this technique. The houses on the left, the boats in the foreground and parts of the sky were drawn with a pen on the white ground, but the rest was covered with ink and then scratched through when the ink dried.

Fig. 36. White scratchboard with pen and ink

You can obtain strong textural effects with black scratchboard. Note the rough appearance of the blocks of stone in the walls in Fig. 37, the texture of the stones in the quay and even the suggested surge of the incoming tide. The over-all effect resembles a woodcut somewhat, and engravers in wood often start with scratchboard sketches.

There is, of course, no reason why you can't frame a scratchboard drawing, but generally you will use this medium as a means to an end. The striking black-and-white effect reproduces very well in print. That is why it is a favorite method of book and magazine illustrators and for use in educational publications.

Corrections on either black or white board are easy to make. Simply ink out any mistakes with a brush, and then rework when the ink dries. Scratchboard is fairly expensive, but you generally

Fig. 37. Black scratchboard with pen and ink

"work small." And the experience you can gain in the use of black and white will make the expense worth while.

IX

MASTERS OF THE PAST

The desire to express thoughts and ideas in paint goes back many thousands of years to our ancestors who first scrawled with lumps of clay and ore on the roofs of their caves. Since then man, as he has become more civilized, has constantly strived to improve this facility, to express his feelings and thoughts in pictures. The painting skill of early Egyptians had a magical significance—to make secure the afterlives of the dead. The Greeks and Romans painted to beautify their houses and public buildings and to spread their ideas. Gradually the early craftsmen discovered how to paint with water color and tempera. Oil painting was perfected during the fourteenth and fifteenth centuries.

Perhaps the greatest era in the history of painting was the Italian Renaissance. In the fifteenth and sixteenth centuries in Italy there were many geniuses, not only in painting but in every field of human endeavor. One of the most famous Renaissance figures was Leonardo da Vinci (1452-1519). Sketches in his many notebooks show that he predicted the invention of airplanes, submarines, tanks and many other modern machines. Besides this achievement, he was a wonderful painter. If you have a chance to travel to Italy, you will be able to see "The Last Supper," possibly his finest work. This painting has suffered damage from weather, faulty restoration and, finally, bombing. After World War II it appeared to be almost beyond repair. It was covered with mold, and the wall on which it was painted was badly cracked. Thanks to the faithful work of a restorer, however, it now approximates its original condition.

Another giant of the time was Michelangelo. As a great painter working largely in fresco (painting directly onto wet plaster), he produced the masterpieces of the Sistine Chapel in Rome. As an architect, he designed one of the finest ecclesiastical buildings of all time, St. Peter's Cathedral, also in Rome. And as a sculptor, he left us a host of wonderful figures in marble, the execution and sheer physical labor of which dwarf the output of even his most prolific contemporaries!

So remarkable was the output of artistic genius during the Renaissance and the following centuries in many European countries, that an adequate selection of the most important works of art would fill volumes—as indeed it has. The examples given here have been chosen to illustrate some of the points discussed in the earlier chapters on drawing, composition and painting.

A fine example of a work with controlled light and shade is "The Supper at Emmaus" (Plate 2) by the Italian Caravaggio. Jesus, resurrected, is just making Himself known to two of his disciples. How wonderfully Caravaggio has caught this moment! The carefully restricted lighting from the left side brilliantly emphasizes not only the face of Jesus but also the illuminated figure on the right, who expresses surprise and wonder with his outstretched arms. Notice particularly the beautifully foreshortened left hand coming toward you and the treatment of the food.

Caravaggio was a gifted exponent of "chiaroscuro," the control of light and shade. He loved to illuminate his pictures dramatically with a rather small source of light, and then to pick it up again in the highlighted figures. Notice the subtlety of the light reflected from the white tablecloth onto the profile of the figure with his back toward the viewer.

"The Supper at Emmaus" also gives a wonderful lesson in tone control. All too often in an interior scene the shadows away from the light are not sufficiently deep. Look again at this picture and see how Caravaggio treats such shadows. Not only does he achieve a great feeling of reality, but his picture also has a strong dramatic quality.

Many painters were influenced by Caravaggio—among them the Spaniards Ribera and Ribalta as well as Rembrandt. This great Dutch painter also employed a small, restricted source of light combined with his great mastery of shadow. In the "Adoration of

Plate 22. "A Winter Scene" by Hendrick Avercamp (1585-1634)

the Shepherds" for example, Rembrandt's use of light achieves a powerful effect of space and depth.

Now look at Plate 22, "A Winter Scene" by Hendrick Avercamp, a Dutch painter. The Dutch and Flemish artists loved small pictures; the original of this is not much more than 18 inches in diameter. Avercamp has filled this panel with crowds of people moving about. Probably he chose a round shape to suit the fashion of his time.

Notice how Avercamp cleverly leads your eye into the picture by the placing of the tree on the left and one or two figures around the old rotten stump. Then, small groups of figures lead the eye across the ice, past the houses on the left and the right, and finally up to the principal feature, the big chateau standing grandly in the background. To appreciate the sublety of the composition, glance at Fig. 38 for a rough idea of how this particular composition could have failed. The centrally placed tree stops the viewer's eye from moving into the picture and hides the chateau at the back. The strength of the composition is entirely lost.

Fig. 38. Avercamp's composition changed so that the strength and unity is lost

Plate 23. "Flowers in a Vase" by Jan van Huysum (1682-1749)

Another example from the Dutch School is a lovely rendering
of a still life. Plate 23 is by Jan Van Huysum, one of many which he
entitled "Flowers in a Vase." At once you can see his great
control of light and shade. Like the earlier Caravaggio, the artist

116

has not been afraid of making his background extremely dark to set off the delicate tracery of the petals and leaves. This composition is particularly interesting because it appears at first glance to be haphazard. But if you study it, you will see that it falls into a very pleasing shape. Helped by the fallen marigold at the bottom and the little snail, the eye can move freely without an impression of discord. Such men as Van Huysum achieved in these pictures an almost miraculous control of oil painting. If you have a chance to look at the original of this or of a similar painting of the same period (the beginning of the eighteenth century), first stand several paces away from it. Later, after you have enjoyed the composition, go up close and examine the skill of the painter who produced it. In this one you will see tiny drops of water gleaming on the leaves, the veins of the leaves themselves, the soft, semi-transparent texture of the petals, a fly crawling on a leaf and a caterpillar climbing a stem. Such pictures are beautiful testimonies to the craftsmanship of their creators.

Landscape as a subject by itself was one of the last to be exploited by artists. This was largely because patrons demanded either religious subjects or portraits. There was no demand for landscapes as a *genre*. Occasionally through a window or for a background we see bits of landscape, but it was not until the sixteenth and seventeenth centuries that the Dutch painters made landscape a specialty.

We have already studied some landscapes in the chapter on oil painting. Hobbema's "The Avenue, Middelharnis" is a rather small canvas. Hobbema has caught most wonderfully the peace and quiet of the Dutch countryside of his time. Although he seems to have disobeyed the rule against symmetry—the avenue of trees is centrally placed—he has effectively broken this symmetry in many ways. In the right foreground a peasant is trimming bushes in his garden; in the left foreground there is a heavy patch of undergrowth and several dark trees. In the right middle distance are a farmhouse and still more trees, and there are clouds in the sky. Notice particularly the large fluffy cloud rising on the right. Together, these objects provide the spatial diversity usually lacking in a symmetrical composition.

Fig. 39 shows the wrong way to treat a subject of this type. In this sketch the placement of the avenue to one side seems to split the picture in two. The strong lines of the vanishing treetops, of the trees themselves and of the tracks in the road distract the eye from the rest of the picture.

Fig. 39. The wrong way to treat Hobbema's subject

"The Hay Wain" by John Constable (Plate 17) typifies the English landscape. Constable loved the country with its great trees, sweeping meadows and magnificent skies, all of which he was able to capture so truly. He liked to work with large brushes and sweeping strokes on a red-ochre-tinged canvas. Again notice his daring use of light where the river sweeps past the little house on the left and underneath the trees. Often beginners fail with brightly lighted landscapes because the shadows are either too dead in color or too light. (You have only to look at the sun shining on a tree on a bright day to realize the very great difference in tone between the light and the shadowed portions.)

This composition is masterful because it is so harmonious. If you are painting a river, the result may be an unsatisfactory impression of parallel lines sweeping across and out of the picture. Not only has Constable brought your eye to rest on the hay wain and the tired horses, but his treatment of the curving river bank holds your eye in the picture. The tiny figure of the dog has its place, too. Put your finger over it for a second and you will see how it enhances the strength of the picture. One of Constable's greatest skills is his ability to draw the eye not only into the picture but away and off toward the far distant horizon. You can almost feel yourself wandering over the flat meadow, beyond the river, through the trees and across the gently rising ground beyond. You can almost see the great soft-bellied massive clouds. Again, contrast "The Hay Wain" with "The Avenue, Middelharnis."

Now we come to the French Impressionists. We have already studied "Le Louvre, Matin, Neige" (Plate 18) by Camille Pissarro. Men such as Pissarro and his contemporaries, Sisley and Monet, gave us a completely new vision of color. As we mentioned earlier, they liked to work with the complementary theory of harmony. They also found ways to imbue shadows with warmth and achieved brilliant, kaleidoscopic displays of pure color in their light passages.

The next of our illustrations is a portrait by Edgar Degas, that of Carlo Pelegrini (Plate 24). It is interesting to compare it with other portraits you may see. Degas did not attempt to give a photographic likeness of his subject, but rather to show him in a characteristic attitude. Look at the picture of this man, the way he is holding his hand, the angle of the head, the left hand holding his hat behind his back and the stance of the feet. From these mannerisms you can grasp more about his character than you could from a more conventional portrait.

Plate 24. "Carlo Pelegrini" by Edgar Degas (1834-1917)
© by S.P.A.D.E.M., Paris

120

X

MODERN ART

The work of many modern artists may bewilder viewers. Yet these painters, too, are striving to extend our experience through the visual arts. Although specific works are not always easy to understand, they represent attempts to capture emotion and thought on canvas. Explosive as the results sometimes are, such works can be extremely effective.

Modern painting really begins with the last years of Paul Cézanne's life (1839–1906) and was profoundly influenced by him. The leader of the post-Impressionists, he sought to interpret natural phenomena from new viewpoints or perspectives, resulting in revolutionary kinds of spatial relationships, in both form and color. His concern with the play of flat planes against one another, the transition of tone and color and the use of the vertical as a means of creating depth is best exemplified in his still lifes, such as the one shown in Plate 25. This technique of transforming natural shapes into geometric forms as an influence for those who followed him, such as the Cubists, can easily be seen. Other post-Impressionists of importance, all of whom developed techniques that were reactionary against the Impressionists, included Vincent Van Gogh (1853–90), Paul Gauguin (1848–1903), Georges Seurat (1859–91), Odilon Redon (1840–1916), and Théodore Rousseau (1812–67).

In the early years of the 20th century a short-lived but important movement appeared—Fauvism, led by Henri Matisse (1869–

Plate 25. "Still Life" by Paul Cézanne (1839-1906)
National Gallery of Art, Washington, D.C. Chester Dale Collection

1954). This basically expressionistic trend is seen in Matisse's "Dance" (Plate 26) where distortion of form was bold and obvious. Matisse, Raoul Dufy (1877–1953), Georges Rouault (1871–1958) and others produced works that exhibited an unprecedented freedom of design and color that has had lasting effects on painting.

Probably the single most revolutionary trend is Cubism which appeared first in Pablo Picasso's (1881–   ) "Les Demoiselles d'Avignon" (Plate 27) which clearly shows the major elements of Cubism—the influence of African sculpture and geometric forms. Picasso has continued to be one of the greatest innovators in almost every art form. Georges Braque (1882–1963) was the real leader of the Cubists and the most important other members were Marcel Duchamp (1887–   ), Fernand Léger (1881–1955) and Juan Gris (1887–1927).

Braque's simultaneous portrayals of more than one view of three-dimensional objects is obvious in his "Still Life: The Table" (Plate 28). Compare this with Cézanne's still life—find not only the similarities but the points of departure.

In other parts of Europe, such as Germany, there came into being movements generally known as Expressionism. Oskar Kokoschka (1886–   ), Edvard Munch (1863–1944), Paul Klee (1879–1940) and Lyonel Feininger (1871–1956) were all representative of various forms of Expressionism. Kokoschka's "Self Portrait" (Plate 29) exhibits one of the major elements of this group—the distortion of reality in order to express an inner self.

Plate 26. "Dance" by Henri Matisse (1869-1954)

Collection, The Museum of Modern Art, New York. Gift of Nelson A. Rockefeller in honor of Alfred H. Barr, Jr.

123

Plate 27. "Les Demoiselles d'Avignon" by Pablo Picasso (1881-   )
Collection, The Museum of Modern Art, New York

Notice the tension in the hand and face. This portrait well illustrates the influence of the 16th-century Spanish painter El Greco, who was an inspiration for the expressionistic painters.

Feininger's "The Steamer Odin, II" (Plate 30) exhibits a geometric style that is present in almost all of his work. He found the forms of boats and buildings best suited to his technique and used them to suggest light rays and architectural forms.

During the 1920's and 30's there developed another new concept of painting—Surrealism. The most prominent members of this movement were Salvador Dali (1904–   ), Yves Tanguy (1900–1955), Max Ernst (1891–   ), and Joan Miró (1893–   ). These painters sought to express the subconscious mind and were greatly influenced by Freudian principles. The Surrealists all had one main aim—to shock the viewer. They borrowed heavily from dreams and fantasy and combined the products of the imaginative mind with everyday objects and environments. (See Joan Miró's "Acrobats In Garden At Night" on the front cover.)

By the mid-1940's the next important movement had begun—Abstract Expressionism. Important because it was the first major trend in modern painting to originate in the United States with a strong influence on European art, it is often referred to as the New York School. Because the very *act* of painting was crucial to its precepts, it was known popularly as "action painting." Some of its major proponents were Jackson Pollock (1912–1956), Willem de

Plate 28. "Still Life: The Table" by Georges Braque (1882-1963)
National Gallery of Art, Washington, D.C.

Plate 29. "Self Portrait"
by Oskar Kokoschka
(1886-)

Kooning (1904–   ), Robert Motherwell (1915–   ) (Plate 31),
Franz Kline (1910–62), Mark Rothko (1903–   ).

Pollock, whose work exhibits the influence of many previous
movements, developed an extremely abstract style. He painted
with the "drip" technique, literally dripping, dribbling and
spattering the paint on great canvases, and produced works that
were a source of controversy. The question, "Is this art?" was
asked by artists and nonartists alike. However, his paintings hang
in major museums and he, like many of his pedecessors, is gradu-

Plate 30. "The Steamer Odin, II" by Lyonel Feininger (1871-1956)

Collection, The Museum of Modern Art, New York. Acquired through the Lillie P. Bliss Bequest

Plate 31. "The Voyage" by Robert Motherwell (1915-   )

Collection, The Museum of Modern Art, New York. Gift of Mrs. John D. Rockefeller, 3rd

ally becoming recognized as an important artist and an expression of his time.

Other influential trends in painting appeared in the United States during the late 1950's and 1960's—chief among them Pop Art and Op Art. Pop Art involves the conversion of such popular "arts" as comic strips, posters and other commercial arts, including silk screens, into fine art. The chief Pop artist is Andy

Plate 32. "That Which Is Seen" by Richard Anuszkiewicz
Sidney Janis Gallery, New York

Warhol. Shortly after Pop Art took hold, "Op Art" made its appearance. Op Art, short for optical art, is based on optical illusions of line and color and has a geometric or draughtmanship quality as can be seen in Plate 32, Richard Anuszkiewicz's "That Which Is Seen." Devoid of emotion or expression of the artist in any way, it is essentially a revolt against the earlier Abstract Expressionism.

During this period also "Minimal Art" became important. This trend aims at the reduction of art to basic shapes and colors. For instance, a large white-painted canvas might have a single white stripe running through it, or a black-painted canvas a small blacker circle.

Hand in hand with new art movements have come new materials. Often in order for an artist to express his ideas, he needs certain properties in his medium. Out of this need, experiments in the paints themselves develop.

In recent years, water-soluble plastic media (acrylics) have gained widespread popularity among artists and have greatly affected trends in modern painting. Quick-drying, the new acrylics allow *speed* in working, which has freed the artist from many technical problems.

Actually, modern painting has had two great effects. For instance, through the apparent simplicity of its techniques and materials, nonartists have often been encouraged to "try their hand." Moreover, the new art has succeeded in arousing an interest in art in the general public. Nonrepresentational and primitive art can well serve as an inspiration for *you* to take up brush in hand and paint to your heart's content.

INDEX